Idioms and Phrases

Idioms and Phrases

Dr. Silvia M. Fernandez

Commonwealth

Idioms and Phrases

Edition : 2023

ISBN 978-81-311-0235-0

Published by **:**
COMMONWEALTH PUBLISHERS (P) LTD.
4831/24, Govind Lane,
Ansari Road, Darya Ganj,
New Delhi - 110002
Ph. : 23272541, 23242541
e-mail : commonwealthpublishers2016@gmail.com

Distributed by :
ARJUN PUBLISHING HOUSE
4831/24, Govind Lane,
Ansari Road, Darya Ganj,
New Delhi - 110002
Ph. : 23272541, 23242541
e-mail : arjunbooks2001@gmail.com

Laser Typesetting by :
Dimple Computers
Delhi

Printed at :
Milan Enterprises
Delhi

Preface

Idioms and phrases are literal expressions which add colour to the language. An idiom is a form of expression, construction, phrase etc., peculiar to a language, a peculiarity of phraseology approved by usage and often having a meaning other than its grammatical or logical one, while a phrase is a group of words that functions as a single unit in the syntax of a sentence. Every language contains such idioms and phrases whether or not they are noted and explained clearly by the grammarians. English is full of many such idiomatic and phraseological expressions.

There are many works in English dealing with idioms and phrases, some of which merely give meanings and some contain etymological explanations and other particulars. A book of such works is a desideratum in English to help the young writers in this great language. The present volume is a small effort in that direction. It is hoped that it would help young scholars to develop in-depth knowledge of idioms and phrases commonly used in English.

Dr. Silvia M. Fernandez

Contents

1

Introduction to Idioms and Phrases

An idiom is a term or phrase whose meaning cannot be deduced from the literal definitions and the arrangement of its parts, but refers instead to a figurative meaning that is known only through common use. In linguistics, idioms are widely assumed to be figures of speech that contradict the principle of compositionality; however, this has shown to be a subject of debate. It may be better to refer to idioms as John Saeed does: words collocated together happen to become fossilised, becoming fixed over time. This collocation — words commonly used in a group — changes the definition of each of the words that exist. As an expression, the word-group becomes a team, so to speak. That is, the collocated words develop a specialised meaning as a whole and an idiom is born e.g. He really threw me a curve when on our first date he asked if I could pay for the dinner. Note, in some cultures, when a man and a woman are courting each other, the male is traditionally the one who takes up the bill or pays the bill; however, times change and in many modern societies, a lot of couples go Dutch (yet another idiom).

In the English expression to kick the bucket, for example, a listener knowing only the meaning of kick and bucket would be unable to deduce the expression's actual meaning, which is to die. Although it can refer literally to the act of striking a specific bucket with a foot, native speakers rarely use it that way. It cannot be directly translated to other languages - for example, the same expression in Polish is kopnac w kalendarz (to kick the calendar), with the calendar being as detached from its usual meaning as the bucket in the English phrase is. The same expression in Dutch is het loodje leggen, which is entirely different from the English expression, too. Other expressions include break a leg and fit as a fiddle. It is estimated that William Shakespeare coined over 9,000 idioms still in use today.

Idioms hence tend to confuse those not already familiar with them; students of a new language must learn its idiomatic expressions the way they learn its other vocabulary. Many natural language words have idiomatic origins, but have been sufficiently assimilated so that their figurative senses have been lost.

IDIOMS AND CULTURE

An idiom is generally a colloquial metaphor - a term which requires some foundational knowledge, information, or experience, to use only within a culture where parties must have common reference. Idioms are therefore not considered a part of the language, but rather a part of the culture. As cultures are typically localised, idioms are more often not useful for outside of that local context. However some idioms can be more universally used than others, and they can be easily translated, metaphorical meaning can be more easily deduced.

The most common idioms can have deep roots, date back many centuries, and be traceable across many languages. Many have translations in other languages, and tend to become international.

While many idioms are clearly based in conceptual metaphors such as "time as a substance", "time as a path", "love as war" or "up is more", the idioms themselves are often not particularly essential, even when the metaphors themselves are. For example, "spend time", "battle of the sexes", and "back in the day" are idiomatic and based in essential metaphors. These "deep metaphors" and their relationship to human cognition are discussed by George Lakoff and Mark Johnson in their 1980 book Metaphors We Live By.

In forms like "profits are up", the metaphor is carried by "up" itself. The phrase "profits are up" is not itself an idiom. Practically anything measurable can be used in place of "profits": "crime is up", "satisfaction is up", "complaints are up" etc. Truly essential idioms generally involve prepositions, for example "out of" or "turn into".

Interestingly, many Chinese characters are likewise idiomatic constructs, as their meanings are more often not traceable to a literal (i.e. pictographic) meaning of their assembled parts, or radicals. Because all characters are composed from a relatively small base of about 214 radicals, their assembled meanings follow several different modes of interpretation - from the pictographic to the metaphorical to those whose original meaning has been lost in history. It may be a feature that helps everyday life.

PARLANCE

"Idiom" can also refer to the characteristic manner of speaking in a language, also called its parlance. An utterance consistent with a language's parlance is described as idiomatic. For example, "I have hunger" is idiomatic in several European languages if translated literally, but the usual English idiom is "I am hungry".

This sense is also carried over to programming languages, where the former sense does not apply, as an expression or statement in a programming language can generally have only one meaning. For example, in Haskell, it is possible to apply a function to all members of a list using recursion, but it is more idiomatic to use the higher-order function map.

Computer Science

In computer science, an idiom is a low-level pattern that addresses a problem common in a particular programming language. An idiom describes how to implement particular aspects of components or the relationships between them using the features of the given language.

For instance, in C source code one might see while(*a++ = *b++);, which copies characters from b to a until the null character ('\0') is encountered.

This is an idiom in that a C programmer on seeing it does not need to mentally parse what it might mean, although in this case the effect of the code can be deduced from the literal syntax and C's order of operations.

PHRASE

In grammar, a phrase is a group of words that functions as a single unit in the syntax of a sentence.

For example the house at the end of the street is a phrase. It acts like a noun. It contains the phrase at the end of the street, a prepositional phrase which acts like an adjective. Most phrases have a or central word which defines the type of phrase. This word is called the head of the phrase. In English the head is often the first word of the phrase. Some phrases, however, can be headless. For example, the rich is a noun phrase composed of a determiner and an adjective, but no noun.

Phrases may be classified by the type of head they take

— Prepositional phrase (PP) with a preposition as head (e.g. in love, over the rainbow). Languages that use postpositions instead have postpositional phrases. The two types are sometimes commonly referred to as adpositional phrases.

— Noun phrase (NP) with a noun as head (e.g. the black cat, a cat on the mat)

— Verb phrase (VP) with a verb as head (e.g. eat cheese, jump up and down)

— Adjectival phrase with an adjective as head (e.g. full of toys)

— Adverbial phrase with adverb as head (e.g. very carefully)

Formal Definition

A phrase is a syntactic structure which has syntactic properties derived from its head.

Complexity

A complex phrase consists of several words, whereas a simple phrase consists of only one word. This terminology is especially often used with verb phrases:

— simple past and present are simple verb, which require just one verb

— complex verb have one or two aspects added, hence require additional two or three words

"Complex", which is phrase-level, is often confused with "compound", which is word-level. However, there are certain phenomena that formally seem to be phrases but semantically are more like compounds, like "women's magazines", which has the form of a possessive noun phrase, but which refers (just like a compound) to one specific lexeme (i.e. a magazine for women and not some magazine owned by a woman).

2

Noun Phrase

A noun phrase comprises a noun (obviously) and any associated modifiers:

— The long and winding road

— A noun phrase

— any associated modifiers

In grammatical theory, a noun phrase (abbreviated NP) is a phrase whose head is a noun or a pronoun, optionally accompanied by a set of modifiers.

FORM

Noun phrases normally consist of a head noun, which is optionally modified ("premodified" If the modifier is placed before the noun; "postmodified" if the modifier is placed after the noun). Possible modifiers include:

— determiners: articles (the, a), demonstratives (this, that), numerals (two, five, etc.), possessives (my, their, etc.), and quantifiers (some, many, etc.). In English, determiners are usually placed before the noun;

— adjectives (the red ball); or

— complements, in the form of a prepositional phrase (such as: the student of physics), or a That-clause (the claim that the earth is round);

— modifiers; premodifiers if placed before the noun and usually either as nouns (the university student) or adjectives (the beautiful lady), or postmodifiers if placed after the noun. A postmodifier may be either a prepositional phrase (the man with long hair) or a relative clause (the house where I live). The difference between modifiers and complements is that complements complete the meaning of the noun; complements are necessary, whereas modifiers are optional because they just give additional information about the noun.

That noun phrases can be headed by elements other than nouns - for instance, pronouns (They came) or determiners ((I'll take these)) - has given rise to the postulation of a Determiner phrase instead of a noun phrase. The English language is not as permissive as some other languages, with regard to possible heads of noun phrases. German, for instance, allows adjectives as heads of noun phrases, as in Gib mir die alten: Give me the olds (= old ones).

Noun phrases can make use of an apposition structure. This means that the elements in the noun phrase are not in a head-modifier relationship, but in a relation of equality. An example of this is I, Caesar, declare ..., where "Caesar" and "I" do not modify each other.

NOUN PHRASE AS A GRAMMATICAL UNIT

In English, for some purposes, noun phrases can be

treated as single grammatical units. This is most noticeable in the syntax of the English genitive case. In a phrase such as The king of Sparta's wife, the possessive clitic "-'s" is not added to the king who actually has the wife, but instead to Sparta, as the end of the whole phrase. The clitic modifies the entire phrase the king of Sparta.

Grammatical Function

Noun phrases are prototypically used for acts of reference as in "The blonde girl shouts" or "She kissed the man". Also possible, but found less often, is the use of noun phrases for predication, as in "Suzy is a blonde girl". Note that in English the use of the copula is indicates the use of a noun phrase as predicate, but other languages may not require the use of the copula. Finally, noun phrases are used for identifications like "The murderer was the butler", where no ascription is talking place. The possibility for a noun phrase to play the role of subject and predicate leads to the constructions of syllogisms.

Cross-linguistic Observations

Noun phrases are very common cross-linguistically, but some languages like Tuscarora and Cayuga have been argued to lack this category.

The modifiers that accompany a noun can take any number of forms and combination of forms: adjectives, of course ("the tall and brilliant professor"); a participial phrase ("the road following the edge of the frozen lake"); an infinitive phrase ("the first man to walk on the moon"); a modifying clause ("the presentation that he had made the day before"); and prepositional phrases ("the building next to the lodge, over by the highway"). Usually, a noun phrase will be all of a piece, all the words that compose it being contiguous with the noun itself. It is possible, however, for a noun phrase to be broken, to become what we call discontinuous. Sometimes part of the noun phrase is delayed until the end of the sentence so that that portion of the phrase (usually modifying phrases - participial or prepositional) can receive end weight or focus. In our first example, for instance.

— Several accidents have been reported involving passengers falling from trains we could have put the entire noun phrase together: "Several accidents involving passengers falling from trains have been reported recently." Shifting the modifying phrases of the red-colored part of the phrase to the end puts additional emphasis on that part. Here are some other examples:

— A rumor circulated among the staff that he was being promoted to Vice President. (instead of "A rumor that he was being promoted to Vice President circulated among the staff.")

— The time had come to stop spending money foolishly and to put something away for the future . (instead of "The time to stop spending money foolishly and to put something away for the future had come.")

— That hard drive was faulty that you sold me. (instead of "That hard drive that you sold me was faulty.")

— What business is it of yours? (instead of "What business of yours is it? ")

Clearly, there is nothing inherently wrong with a discontinuous noun phrase. One very good reason for a discontinuous noun phrase is to achieve a balance between a subject and its predicate:

— The story is told that he was once a soldier in French Foreign Legion.

Without the discontinuous noun phrase in the sentence above, we end up with a twelve-word subject, a linking verb, and a one-word predicate - sort of lop-sided.

One thing you want to watch out for with noun phrases is the long compound noun phrase. This is sometimes called the "stacked noun phrase" or "packed noun phrase." It is common to find one noun modifying another: student body, book cover, water commission. But when we create a long string of such attributive nouns or modifiers, we create difficulties:

— People who author web-pages have become aware of what is now known as the uniform resource locator protocol problem.

The difficulty we have here is knowing what is modifying what. Also, the reader keeps expecting the string to end, so the energy of the sentence (and our attention) dwindles into a series of false endings. Such phrases are a particular temptation in technical writing. Usually, the solution to an overly extended compound noun phrase is to take the last noun of the series and liberate it from the rest of the string (putting it at the beginning of the sentence) and then to turn at least one of the modifying nouns into a prepositional phrase:

— The problem with the protocol of uniform resource locators is now recognised by people who author web-pages as. . . .

A vocative - an addressed person's name or substitute name - is often a single word but sometimes takes the form of a noun phrase. A vocative is always treated as a parenthetical element and is thus set off from the rest of the sentence with a comma or a pair of commas (if it appears within the flow of a sentence). When vocatives are proper nouns (usually the case), they are also referred to as "nouns of address." Vocatives are like adverbs: they can pop up almost anywhere in the sentence. Do not, however, get into the habit of throwing commas at people's names; unless the name refers to someone who is actually being addressed, it is not a vocative and will not necessarily be parenthetical:

— He told Jorge to turn the boat around.

— Jorge, turn the boat around

Quirk and Greenbaum enumerate four different kinds of vocatives:

1. *Single names, with or without a title:* Jorge, Mr. Valdez, Dr. Valdez, Uncle, Grandma. Dr. Valdez, will you please address the graduates?

2. *The personal pronoun you (not a polite form of address):* You, put down that gun! The second person pronoun is sometimes combined with other words (but the result is often rather rude

and is never used in formal prose ["You over there, hurry up!" "You with the purple hair and silver nose rings, get back in line!"]) The indefinite pronouns can also serve as a vocative: Call an ambulance, somebody! Quick, anybody! Give me a hand!

3. Appellatives (what we call people) of endearment ("Darling," "Sweetheart," "My dear," "Love") Come sit next to me, my dear.; of respect ("Sir," "Madam," "Your Honor," "Ladies and gentlemen") I would ask you, Sir, never to do that again.; of profession or status ("Professor," "Mr. President," "Madam Chairman," "Coach") Please, Coach, let me play for a while.
4. Nominal clause: Whoever is making that noise, stop it now.

Full References

The discussion of the choice of language noted that a single concept is often signaled by a variety of words, each word possessing slightly different connotations. We can indicate that people are less than content by saying they are angry , irate , incensed , perturbed , upset , furious , or mad. The broader our vocabulary, the greater our options and the more precisely we can convey our meaning.

And yet no matter how wide our vocabulary may be, a single word is often insufficient. A single word, by itself, can appear somewhat vague, no matter how specific that word might seem. The term "dog" may be specific compared to "mammal," but it is general compared to "collie." And "collie" is general compared to "Lassie." Then again, many different dogs played Lassie!

Suppose you want to indicate a female person across the room. If you don't know her name, what do you say?

> That girl.

If there were more than one, this alone would be too general. It lacks specificity.

> The girl in the blue Hawaiian shirt...
> The taller of the two cheerleaders by the water cooler...

When a single term will not supply the reference we need, we add terms to focus or limit a more general term. Instead of referring to drugs in a discussion, we might refer to hallucinogenic drugs. We might distinguish between hard drugs and prescription drugs . In so doing we modify the notion of a drug to describe the specific one, or ones, we have in mind.

NOUNS

English teachers commonly identify nouns by their content. They describe nouns as words that "identify people, places, or things," as well as feelings or ideas-words like salesman , farm , balcony , bicycle , and trust. If you can usually put the word a or the before a word, it's a noun. If you can make the word plural or singular, it's a noun. But don't worry...all that is needed at the moment is a sense of what a noun might be.

Noun Pre-Modifiers

What if a single noun isn't specific enough for our purposes? How then do we modify a noun to construct a more specific reference?

English places modifiers before a noun. Here we indicate the noun that is at the center of a noun phrase by an asterisk (*) and modifiers by arrows pointed toward the noun they modify.

white	*house*
→	*
large	*man*
→	*

Modification is a somewhat technical term in linguistics. It does not mean to change something, as when we "modify" a car or dress. To modify means to limit, restrict, characterise, or otherwise focus meaning. We use this meaning throughout the discussion here.

Modifiers before the noun are called pre-modifiers. All of the pre-modifiers that are present and the noun together form a noun phrase .

Noun	Phrase
pre-modifiers	*noun*
→	*

By contrast, languages such as Spanish and French place modifiers after the noun

casa blanca	*white house*
* ←	

homme grand *big man*

* ←

The most common pre-modifiers are adjectives, such as red , long , hot . Other types of words often play this same role. Not only articles

the *water*

→ *

but also verbs

running water

→ *

and possessive pronouns

her *thoughts*

← *

Premodifiers limit the reference in a wide variety of ways.

Order:	second, last
Location:	kitchen, westerly
Source or Origin:	Canadian
Color:	red, dark
Smell:	acrid, scented
Material:	metal, oak
Size:	large, 5-inch
Weight:	heavy
Luster:	shiny, dull

A number of pre-modifiers must appear first if they appear at all.

Specification:	a, the, every

Designation: this, that, those, these

Ownership/Possessive: my, your, its, their, Mary's

Number: one, many

These words typically signal the beginning of a noun phrase. Some noun phrases are short:

the *table*

→ *

Some are long:

the second shiny red Swedish touring sedan

---------------------------> *

a large smelly red Irish setter

----------------------> *

my carved green Venetian glass salad bowl

---> *

the three old Democratic legislators

--------------------> *

Notice that each construction would function as a single unit within a sentence.

The noun phrase is the most common unit in English sentences. That prevalence can be seen in the following excerpt from an example from the section on the choice of language:

— The stock market's summer swoon turned into a dramatic rout

— Monday as the Dow Jones industrial average plunged.

* --------------> *

— The stock market's summer swoon turned into a dramatic rout ----------->

* --------> *

— Monday as the Dow Jones industrial average plunged.

* ------------> *

To appreciate the rich possibilities of pre-modifiers, you have only to see how much you can expand a premodifier in a noun phrase:

— the book

— the history book

— the American history book

— the illustrated American history book

— the recent illustrated American history book

— the recent controversial illustrated American history book

— the recent controversial illustrated leather bound American history book

Noun Post-Modifiers

We were all taught about pre -modifiers: adjectives appearing before a noun in school. Teachers rarely speak as much about adding words after the initial reference. Just as we find pre -modifiers, we also find post -modifiers-modifiers coming after a noun.

The most common post-modifier is prepositional phrases:

the book on the table

→ * ←

civil conflict in Africa

→ * ←

the Senate of the United States

→ * ----->

Post-modifiers can be short

a dream deferred

→ * ←

or long, as in Martin Luther King Jr.'s reference to

a dream that one day on the red hills of Georgia the sons of former slaves

→ * <---------------

and the sons of former slaveowners will be able to sit down together

----

at a table of brotherhood.

What does King have? A dream? No. He has a specific dream. Once we are sensitive to the existence of noun phrases, we recognise a relatively simple structure to the sentence. Here we recognise a noun phrase with a very long post-modifier-thirty-two words to be exact.

Post-modifiers commonly answer the traditional news reporting questions of who, what, where, when, how, or why. Noun post-modifiers commonly take the following forms:

prepositional phrase the dog in the store

→ * <——

_ing phrase	the girl running to the store → * <--------------
_ed past tense	the man wanted by the police → * <-------------
wh - clauses	the house where I was born → * <-------
that/which clauses	the thought that I had yesterday → * <----

If you see a preposition, *wh - word* (*which, who, when where*), -ing verb form, or that or which after a noun, you can suspect a post-modifier and the completion of a noun phrase.

The noun together with all pre- and post-modifiers constitutes a single unit, a noun phrase that indicates the complete reference. Any agreement in terms of singular/plural is with the noun at the center.

The boys on top of the house are ....

→ * <-------------

Here the noun at the center of the noun phrase is plural, so a plural form of the verb is called for (not a singular form to agree with the singular house) .

Pronoun Test

In school, we were taught that pronouns replaced nouns. Not so. Pronouns replace complete noun phrases. Pronoun replacement thus offers a test of a complete noun phrase. Consider:

The boy ate the apple in the pie.

What did he eat?

The boy ate the apple in the pie.

→ * <------

Want proof? Introduce the pronoun "it" into the sentence. If a pronoun truly replaces a noun, we'd get

*The boy ate the it in the pie.

No native speaker would say that! They'd say

The boy ate it.

The pronoun replaces the complete noun phrase, *the apple in the pie.*

This pronoun substitution test can be particualrly useful. Not all prepositional phrases after a noun are necessarily part of the noun phrase - they could be later predicate or sentence modifiers. In other words, we must not only identify noun phrases, we must parse out other material, and in that act recognise broader aspects of sentence structure.

The web page on distinguishing sentence and predicate modifiers discusses the three sentences:

1. The boy ate the apple in the pie.
2. The boy ate the apple in the summer.
3. The boy ate the apple in a hurry.

Only the first includes a noun phrase longer than two words: the apple in the pie.

Boxes Within Boxes: Testing for a Complete Noun Phrase

The goal of reading, we noted above, is not to recognise grammatical features, but to find meaning. The goal is not to break a sentence or part of a sentence into as small pieces as possible, but to break it into chunks in such a way that fosters the discovery of meaning.

Consider one of the examples above of a prepositional phrase as a post-modifier:

the book on the table

Book is a noun at the center of the noun phrase. But table is also a noun. If we analyse the noun phrase completely, on all levels, we find:

the *book* on the table

→ * <---------

on the *table*

→ *

We can have prepositional phrase within prepositional phrase within prepositional phrases:

..the book on the table in the kitchen...

→ * <---------

on the table in the kitchen...

→ * <---------

in the kitchen ...

→ *

We don't want to recognise every little noun phrase. We want to recognise the larger ones that shape the meaning. The book is not "on the table." The book is "on the table in the kitchen."

3

Prepositional Phrase

A prepositional phrase consists of a preposition, a noun or pronoun that serves as the object of the preposition, and, more often than not, an adjective or two that modifies the object. Ernest Hemingway apparently fell in love with the rhythms of his prepositional phrases at the beginning of his short story "Hills Like White Elephants":

The hills across the valley of the Ebro were long and white. On this side there was no shade and no trees and the station was between two lines of rails in the sun. Close against the side of the station there was the warm shadow of the building and a curtain, made of strings of bamboo beads, hung across the open door into the bar, to keep out flies. The American and the girl with him sat at a table in the shade, outside the building. It was very hot and the express from Barcelona would come in forty minutes. It stopped at this junction for two minutes and went on to Madrid.

Prepositional phrases usually tell when or where: "in forty minutes," "in the sun, against the side, etc." Prepositional phrases can perform other functions, however: Except *Jo,* the children were remarkably like *their father*.

A prepositional phrase at the beginning of a sentence constitutes an introductory modifier, which is usually a signal for a comma. However, unless an introductory prepositional phrase is unusually long, we seldom need to follow it with a comma.

You may have learned that ending a sentence with a preposition is a serious breach of grammatical etiquette. It doesn't take a grammarian to spot a sentence-ending preposition, so this is an easy rule to get caught up on (!). Although it is often easy to remedy the offending preposition, sometimes it isn't, and repair efforts sometimes result in a clumsy sentence. Based on shaky historical precedent, the rule itself is a latecomer to the rules of writing. Those who dislike the rule are fond of recalling Churchill's rejoinder: <"That is nonsense up with which I shall not put." We should also remember the child's complaint: "What did you bring that book that I don't like to be read to out of up for?"

BUILDING SENTENCES WITH PREPOSITIONAL PHRASES

Prepositional phrases may do more than just add minor details to a sentence: they may, in fact, be needed for a sentence to make sense. Consider the vagueness of this sentence without prepositional phrases:

— The workers gather a rich variety and distribute it.

— Now see how the sentence comes into focus when we add prepositional phrases:

— From many sources, the workers at the Community Food Bank gather a rich variety of surplus and unsalable food and distribute it to soup kitchens, day-care centers, and homes for the elderly.

Notice how these added prepositional phrases give us more information about certain nouns and verbs in the sentence:

— Which workers?
The workers *at the Community Food Bank.*

— What did they gather?
A rich variety *of surplus and unsalable food.*

— Where did they gather the food?
From many sources.

— Who did they distribute it to?
To soup kitchens, day-care centers, and homes for the elderly.

Like the other simple modifiers, prepositional phrases are not merely ornaments; they add details that can help us *understand* a sentence.

Practice : Building with simple modifiers
Use adjectives, adverbs, and prepositional phrases to expand the sentence below. Add details that answer the questions in parentheses and make the sentence more interesting and informative.

Jenny stood, raised her shotgun, aimed, and fired.

(*Where did Jenny stand? How did she aim? What did she fire at?*)

There are, of course, no single correct answers to the questions in parentheses. Sentence-expanding exercises such as this one encourage you to use your imagination to build original sentences.

Common Prepositions

about	behind	except	outside
above	below	for	over
across	beneath	from	past
after	beside	in	through
against	between	inside	to
along	beyond	into	under
among	by	near	until
around	despite	of	up
at	down	off	with
before	during	on	without

IDENTIFYING PREPOSITIONAL PHRASES

The following paragraph is John Steinbeck's famous novel *The Grapes of Wrath's,* first published in 1939. As you read this paragraph, see if you can identify all of the prepositional phrases used by Steinbeck to convey the dramatic return of rain after a long, painful drought. When you're done, compare your results with the second version of the paragraph, in which prepositional phrases are highlighted in bold print.

Original Paragraph by John Steinbeck

Over the high coast mountains and over the valleys the gray clouds marched in from the ocean. The wind blew fiercely and silently, high in the air, and it swished in the brush, and it roared in the forests. The clouds came in brokenly, in puffs, in folds, in gray crags; and they piled in together and settled low over the west. And then the wind stopped and left the clouds deep and solid. The rain began with gust showers, pauses and downpours; and then gradually it settled to a single tempo, small drops and a steady beat, rain that was gray to see through, rain that cut midday light to evening. And at first the dry earth sucked the moisture down and blackened. For two days the earth drank the rain, until the earth was full. Then puddles formed, and in the low places little lakes formed in the fields. The muddy lakes rose higher, and the steady rain whipped the shining water.

At last the mountains were full, and the hillsides spilled into the streams, built them to freshlets, and sent them roaring down the canyons into the valleys. The rain beat on steadily. And the streams and the little rivers edged up to the bank sides and worked at willows and tree roots, bent the willows deep in the current, cut out the roots of cotton-woods and brought down the trees. The muddy water whirled along the bank sides and crept up the banks until at last it spilled over, into the fields, into the orchards, into the cotton patches where the black stems stood. Level fields became lakes, broad and gray, and the rain whipped up the surfaces. Then the water poured over the highways, and cars moved slowly, cutting the water ahead, and leaving a boiling muddy wake behind. The earth whispered under the beat of the rain, and the streams thundered under the churning freshlets.

Steinbeck's Paragraph with Prepositional Phrases in Bold

Over the high coast mountains and over the valleys

the gray clouds marched in from the ocean. The wind blew fiercely and silently, high in the air, and it swished in the brush, and it roared in the forests. The clouds came in brokenly, in puffs, in folds, in gray crags; and they piled in together and settled low over the west. And then the wind stopped and left the clouds deep and solid.

The rain began with gust showers, pauses and downpours; and then gradually it settled to a single tempo, small drops and a steady beat, rain that was gray to see through, rain that cut midday light to evening. And at first the dry earth sucked the moisture down and blackened. For two days the earth drank the rain, until the earth was full. Then puddles formed, and in the low places little lakes formed in the fields.

The muddy lakes rose higher, and the steady rain whipped the shining water. At last the mountains were full, and the hillsides spilled into the streams, built them to freshlets, and sent them roaring down the canyons into the valleys. The rain beat on steadily. And the streams and the little rivers edged up to the bank sides and worked at willows and tree roots, bent the willows deep in the current, cut out the roots of cotton-woods and brought down the trees.

The muddy water whirled along the bank sides and crept up the banks until at last it spilled over, into the fields, into the orchards, into the cotton patches where the black stems stood. Level fields became lakes, broad and gray, and the rain whipped up the surfaces. Then the water poured over the highways, and cars moved slowly, cutting the water ahead, and leaving a boiling muddy wake behind. The earth whispered under the beat of the rain, and the streams thundered under the churning freshlets.

Common Prepositions

about	behind	except	outside
above	below	for	over
across	beneath	from	past
after	beside	in	through
against	between	inside	to
along	beyond	into	under
among	by	near	until
around	despite	of	up
at	down	off	with
before	during	on	without

SENTENCE COMBINING WITH PREPOSITIONAL PHRASES

Combine the sentences in each set into a single clear sentence containing at least one prepositional phrase. Omit words that are needlessly repeated, but don't leave out any important details. If you run into problems, you may find it helpful to review the following pages:

— Adding Prepositional Phrases to the Basic Sentence Unit

— Introduction to Sentence Combining

After you have completed the exercise, compare your new sentences with the original sentences at the bottom of this page. Keep in mind that many combinations are possible, and in some cases you may prefer your own sentences to the original versions.

1. A mouse darted.
   It darted across the salad bar.
   This happened during the luncheon.

2. We traveled this summer.
   We traveled by train.
   We traveled from Biloxi.
   We traveled to Dubuque.

3. The convertible swerved, crashed, and caromed.
   It swerved off the road.
   It crashed through the guardrail.
   It caromed off a maple tree.

4. Mick planted seeds.
   He planted them in his garden.
   He did this after the quarrel.
   The quarrel was with Mr. Jimmy.

5. Grandpa dropped his teeth.
   His teeth were false.
   His teeth dropped into a glass.
   There was prune juice in the glass.

6. Lucy played.
   She was behind the sofa.
   She was with her friend.
   Her friend was imaginary.
   They played for hours.

7. There was a man.
   He wore a chicken costume.
   He dashed across the field.
   He did this before the ballgame.
   The ballgame was on Sunday afternoon.

8. A man stood, looking down.
   He stood upon a railroad bridge.

The bridge was in northern Alabama.
He was looking down into the water.
The water was twenty feet below.
The water was swift.

9. The gray-flannel fog closed off the Salinas Valley.
It was the fog of winter.
The fog was high.
The Salinas Valley was closed off from the sky.
And the Salinas Valley was closed off from all the rest of the world.

10. I climbed to my perch.
I did this one night.
The night was hot.
The night was in the summer.
The night was in 1949.
It was my usual perch.
My perch was in the press box.
The press box was cramped.
The press box was above the stands.
The stands were wooden.
These were the stands of the baseball park.
The baseball park was in Lumberton, North Carolina.

Sample Comibations

1. During the luncheon, a mouse darted across the salad bar.
2. This summer we traveled by train from Biloxi to Dubuque.
3. The convertible swerved off the road, crashed through the guardrail, and caromed off a maple tree.

4. After his quarrel with Mr. Jimmy, Mick planted seeds in his garden.
5. Grandpa dropped his false teeth into a glass of prune juice.
6. Lucy played behind the couch for hours with her imaginary friend.
7. Before the ballgame on Sunday afternoon, a man in a chicken costume dashed across the field.
8. A man stood upon a railroad bridge in northern Alabama, looking down into the swift waters twenty feet below. (Ambrose Bierce, "An Occurrence at Owl Creek Bridge")
9. The high gray-flannel fog of winter closed off the Salinas Valley from the sky and from all the rest of the world. (John Steinbeck, "The Chrysanthemums")
10. One hot night in the summer of 1949, I climbed to my usual perch in the cramped press box above the wooden stands of the baseball park in Lumberton, North Carolina. (Tom Wicker, "Baseball")

ADDING PREPOSITIONAL PHRASES TO THE BASIC SENTENCE UNIT

Like adjectives and adverbs, prepositional phrases add meaning to the nouns and verbs in our sentences. There are two prepositional phrases in the following sentence:

The steamy air *in the kitchen* reeked *of stale beer.*

The first prepositional phrase—*in the kitchen*—modifies the noun *air;* the second—*of stale beer*—

modifies the verb *reeked*. The two phrases provide information that helps us to understand the sentence.

A prepositional phrase has two basic parts: a preposition plus a noun or a pronoun that serves as the object of the preposition. A preposition is a word that shows *how* a noun or a pronoun is related to another word in a sentence. The common prepositions are listed in the table at the bottom of this page.

Prepositional phrases may do more than just add minor details to a sentence: they may, in fact, be needed for a sentence to make sense. Consider the vagueness of this sentence without prepositional phrases:

— The workers gather a rich variety and distribute it.

— Now see how the sentence comes into focus when we add prepositional phrases:

— *From many sources,* the workers *at the Community Food Bank* gather a rich variety *of surplus and unsalable food* and distribute it *to soup kitchens, day-care centers, and homes for the elderly.*

Notice how these added prepositional phrases give us more information about certain nouns and verbs in the sentence:

— Which workers?
The workers *at the Community Food Bank.*

— What did they gather?
A rich variety *of surplus and unsalable food.*

— Where did they gather the food?
From many sources.

— Who did they distribute it to?
To soup kitchens, day-care centers, and homes for the elderly.

Like the other simple modifiers, prepositional phrases are not merely ornaments; they add details that can help us *understand* a sentence.

Building with Simple Modifiers

Use adjectives, adverbs, and prepositional phrases to expand the sentence below. Add details that answer the questions in parentheses and make the sentence more interesting and informative.

> Jenny stood, raised her shotgun, aimed, and fired.
>
> (*Where did Jenny stand? How did she aim? What did she fire at?*)

There are, of course, no single correct answers to the questions in parentheses. Sentence-expanding exercises such as this one encourage you to use your imagination to build original sentences.

Arranging Prepositional Phrases

A prepositional phrase often appears *after* the word it modifies:

— A spaceship *from Venus* landed *in my back yard.*

— However, like adverbs, prepositional phrases that modify verbs can also be found at the very beginning or very end of a sentence:

— *In the morning,* the Venusians mowed my lawn.
The Venusians mowed my lawn *in the morning.*

— In both versions, the prepositional phrase *in the morning* modifies the verb *mowed.*

Not all phrases are this flexible, and so we need to be careful not to confuse our readers by misplacing a prepositional phrase:

— The Venusians swam for two hours after lunch *in my pool.*

— This arrangement gives the idea that the visitors from Venus enjoyed lunch in the pool. If this is not the case, shift the prepositional phrase:

— After lunch, the Venusians swam for two hours *in my pool.*

— The best arrangement is one that is both clear and uncluttered.

Although several prepositional phrases may appear in the same sentence, avoid packing in so many phrases that you confuse the reader. The sentence below, for example, is cluttered and awkward:

— On a rickety stool in one corner of the crowded honky tonk, the folk singer sits playing lonesome songs on his battered old guitar about warm beer, cold women, and long nights on the road.

In this case, the best way to break up the string of phrases is to make two sentences:

— On a rickety stool in one corner of the crowded honky tonk, the folk singer sits hunched over his battered old guitar. He plays lonesome songs about warm beer, cold women, and long nights on the road.

— A *long* sentence is not necessarily an *effective* sentence.

Rearranging Prepositional Phrases

Break up the long string of phrases in the sentence below by creating two sentences. Be sure to include all of the details contained in the original sentence.

Up and down the coast the line of the forest is drawn sharp and clean in the brilliant colors of a wet blue morning in spring on the edge of a seascape of surf and sky and rocks.

Eliminating Needless Modifiers

We can improve our writing by using adjectives, adverbs, and prepositional phrases that *add* to the meaning of sentences. We can also improve our writing by eliminating modifiers that add nothing to the meaning. A good writer does not waste words, so let's cut the clutter.

The following sentence is wordy because some of the modifiers are repetitious or insignificant:

Wordy: The steward was really a very friendly and agreeable man, quite round, rotund, and sleek, with a very costly set of dimples around his terribly pleasant smile.

We can make this sentence more concise (and thus more effective) by cutting out the repetitious and overworked modifiers:

Revised: The steward was an agreeable man, rotund, and sleek, with a costly set of dimples around his smile.

4

Appositive Phrase

An appositive is a re-naming or amplification of a word that immediately precedes it. (An appositive, then is the opposite of an oppositive.) Frequently another kind of phrase will serve in apposition.

— My favorite teacher, a fine chess player in her own right, has won several state-level tournaments. [Noun phrase as appositive]

— The best exercise, walking briskly, is also the least expensive. [Gerund phrase as appositive]

— Tashonda's goal in life, to become an occupational therapist, is within her grasp this year, at last. [Infinitive phrase as appositive]

An appositive is a word placed after another word to explain or identify it. The appositive *always*

— appears after the word it explains or identifies. It is *always* a noun or a pronoun, and the word it explains is *also*

— a noun or pronoun.
ex. My uncle, *a* lawyer, is visiting us.

— My teacher, Miss Marshall, is very strict.

— An appositive phrase consists of the appositive

and its modifiers which may themselves be phrases.

ex. My radio, an old portable, is in the repair shop.

— The boys climbed the mountain, *one of the highest in the West.*

Identifying Appositive Phrases. Underline the appositive phrase in each of the following sentences.

Example: Our house, a brick bungalow, is on Oak Street.

1. Queen Victoria, one of England's greatest monarchs, ruled for sixty-three years.
2. Jane made the salad, a tossed one with French dressing.
3. Harvey Jensen, the pro at the country club, is giving me golf lessons.
4. James Hilton's book, *Lost Horizon*, has been filmed twice.
5. Chemistry, Sue's favorite subject, is easy for her.
6. Jerry is visiting in Peoria, his old home town.
7. Mr. and Mrs. Miller, our neighbors for the past eight years, are moving to Dallas.
8. Have you ever read *The Red Pony*, a novel by John Steinbeck?
9. Groucho Marx, the star of many film comedies, also had his own television show.
10. The boys repaired our television set, an eighteen-year-old portable.
11. The poem, one of Robert Frost's best, is called "The Death of the Hired Man."

12. I can't find my notebook, the one I use for history class.
13. Dick's new suit, a gray flannel one, makes him look much older.
14. We enjoy walking, an exercise which requires no great skill.
15. The theater, an old and drafty one, is nevertheless always crowded.
16. My math teacher, Miss Holmes, has taught for twenty years.
17. The garage, a two-car one, is attached to the house.
18. My sister, a graduate of the University of Iowa, is now studying law.
19. Our dog, a cocker spaniel, is ten years old.
20. Mrs. Norbert, the president of the company, will speak at the dinner

BUILDING SENTENCES WITH APPOSITIVES

An appositive is a word or group of words that identifies or renames another word in a sentence. Appositive constructions offer concise ways of describing or defining a person, place, or thing. Here we will practice building sentences with these economical structures.

From Adjective Clauses to Appositives

Like an adjective clause, an appositive provides more information about a noun. In fact, we may think of an appositive as a simplified adjective clause. Consider, for example, how the following two sentences can be combined:

— Jimbo Gold is a professional magician. Jimbo Gold performed at my daughter's birthday party.

— One way to combine these sentences is to turn the first sentence into an adjective clause:

— Jimbo Gold, who is a professional magician, performed at my daughter's birthday party.

— We also have the option of reducing the adjective clause in this sentence to an appositive; all that we need to do is omit the pronoun *who* and the verb *is*:

— Jimbo Gold, a professional magician, performed at my daughter's birthday party.

— The appositive *a professional magician* serves to identify the subject, *Jimbo Gold*. Reducing an adjective clause to an appositive is one way to cut the clutter in our writing.

However, not all adjective clauses can be shortened to appositives in this fashion: only those that contain a form of the verb to be (*is, are, was, were*).

Arranging Appositives

An appositive most often appears directly after the noun it identifies or renames:

— Arizona Bill, "The Great Benefactor of Mankind," toured Oklahoma with herbal cures and a powerful liniment.

— Note that this appositive, like most, could be omitted without changing the basic meaning of the sentence. In other words, it is nonrestrictive and needs to be set off with a pair of commas.

Occasionally, an appositive may appear in front of a word that it identifies:

— A dark wedge, the eagle hurtled earthward at nearly 200 miles per hour.

— An appositive at the beginning of a sentence is usually followed by a comma.

In each of the examples seen so far, the appositive has referred to the subject of the sentence. However, an appositive may appear before or after *any* noun in a sentence. In the following example, the appositive refers to *roles*, the object of a preposition:

People are summed up largely by the roles they fill in society—wife or husband, soldier or salesperson, student or scientist—and by the qualities that others ascribe to them.

This sentence demonstrates a different way of punctuating appositives—with dashes. When the appositive itself contains commas, setting off the construction with dashes helps to prevent confusion. Using dashes instead of commas also serves to emphasize the appositive.

Placing an appositive at the very end of a sentence is another way to give it special emphasis. Compare these two sentences:

At the far end of the pasture, the most magnificent animal I had ever seen—a white-tailed deer—was cautiously edging toward a salt-lick block.

At the far end of the pasture, the most magnificent animal I had ever seen was cautiously edging toward a salt-lick block—a white-tailed deer.

Whereas the appositive merely interrupts the first sentence, it marks the climax of sentence two.

Punctuating Nonrestrictive and Restrictive Appositives

As we've seen, most appositives are *nonrestrictive*—that is, the information that they add to a sentence is not essential for the sentence to make sense. Nonrestrictive appositives are set off by commas or dashes.

A *restrictive appositive* (like a restrictive adjective clause) is one that cannot be omitted from a sentence without affecting the basic meaning of the sentence. A restrictive appositive should *not* be set off by commas:

— John-Boy's sister Mary Ellen became a nurse after their brother Ben took a job at a lumber mill.

— Because John-Boy has multiple sisters and brothers, the two restrictive appositives make clear *which* sister and *which* brother the writer is talking about. In other words, the two appositives are restrictive, and so they are not set off by commas.

Four Variations

1. *Appositives that Repeat a Noun:* Although an appositive usually *renames* a noun in a sentence, it may instead *repeat* a noun for the sake of clarity and emphasis:

In America, as in anywhere else in the world, we must find *a focus* in our lives at an early age, a focus that is beyond the mechanics of earning a living or coping with a household. (Santha Rama Rau, "An invitation to Serenity")

Notice that the appositive in this sentence is modified by an adjective clause. Adjectives, prepositional phrases, and adjective clauses (in other words, all of the structures that can modify a noun) are often used to add details to an appositive.

2. *Negative Appositives:* Most appositives identify what someone or something *is*, but there are also negative appositives that identify what someone or something *is not*:

— Line managers and production employees, rather than staff specialists, are primarily responsible for quality assurance.

— Negative appositives begin with a word such as *not, never*, or *rather than.*

3. *Multiple Appositives:* Two, three, or even more appositives may appear alongside the same noun:

— Saint Petersburg, a city of almost five-million people, Russia's second-largest and northernmost metropolis, was designed three centuries ago by Peter the Great.

— As long as we don't overwhelm the reader with too much information at one time, a double or triple appositive can be an effective way of adding supplementary details to a sentence.

4. *List Appositives with Pronouns* : A final variation is the list appositive that precedes a pronoun such as *all* or *these* or *everyone*:

   Streets of yellow row houses, the ochre plaster walls of old churches, the crumbling sea-green mansions now occupied by government offices—*all* seem in sharper focus, with their defects hidden by the snow.

   (Leona P. Schecter, "Moscow")

   The word *all* is not essential to the meaning of the sentence: the opening list could serve by itself as the subject. However, the pronoun helps to clarify the subject by drawing the items together before the sentence goes on to make a point about them.

Practice in Using Appositives

As we've seen, an appositive is a word or group of words that concisely identifies or renames another word in a sentence. The exercises on this page offer practice in identifying, building, and revising sentences with appositives.

Identifying Appositives

Some of the sentences below contain adjective clauses; others contain appositives. Identify the adjective clause or appositive in each sentence; then compare your responses with the answers at the end of the exercise.

1. John Reed, an American journalist, helped found the Communist Labor Party in America.

2. My sister, who is a supervisor at Munchies, drives a company car.
3. I took a cookie from Gretel, who is the woodcutter's daughter.
4. I took a cookie from Gretel, the woodcutter's daughter.
5. Og, the King of Bashan, was saved from the flood by climbing onto the roof of the ark.
6. I once saw Margot Fonteyn, the famous ballerina.
7. Elkie Fern, who is a professional botanist, led the kids on a nature hike.
8. Elsa, a good country woman, has a daughter named Ulga.
9. Paul Revere, who was a silversmith and a soldier, is famous for his "midnight ride."
10. I read a biography of Disraeli, the 19th-century statesman and novelist.

Answers

1. appositive: an American journalist
2. adjective clause: who is a supervisor at Munchies
3. adjective clause: who is the woodcutter's daughter
4. appositive: the woodcutter's daughter
5. appositive: the King of Bashan
6. appositive: the famous ballerina
7. adjective clause: who is a professional botanist

8. appositive: a good country woman
9. adjective clause: who was a silversmith and a soldier
10. appositive: the 19th-century statesman and novelist

Building and Revising Sentences with Appositives

Rewrite each of the following sentences (or sets of sentences) according to the instructions in parentheses. (If you run into problems, review Building Sentences with Appositives.) When you're done, compare your responses with the answers at the end of the exercise. Note that in most cases more than one combination is possible.

1. (Combine the two sentences below into a single clear sentence: turn the first sentence into an appositive.

   St. Valentine is the patron saint of lovers. St. Valentine was never married.

2. (Combine the two sentences below by turning the second sentence into an appositive.

   Lewis Carroll is the author of Alice in Wonderland.

   Lewis Carroll was a mathematics lecturer at Oxford University.

3. (Convert the adjective clause—in italics—into an appositive by eliminating the relative pronoun and the verb is.)

   Willie Sarkis, who was a concert pianist in his youth, now plays for tips and drunks at the Rainbow Grill.

4. (Combine the two sentences below by treating the pastoral god of fertility as an appositive.)

   Pan is the pastoral god of fertility.

   He is commonly depicted as a man with goat's horns, ears, and legs.

5. (Combine the three sentences below into a single clear sentence; create an appositive out of the words in italics, and place the appositive at the start of your new sentence.)

   Mr. Bun is a sneaky man.
   Mr. Bun is a sinister man.
   Mr. Bun lingers in the alleys at dawn.
   Mr. Bun creeps along the front walk every evening.

6. (Combine the sentences below by turning the first sentence into an appositive; place it after the word Hawaii, and set it off with dashes.)

   Hawaii is an island far distant from the major sources of pollution.

   The filth in the air over Hawaii has increased dramatically over the past 30 years.

7. (Rewrite the sentence below so that the appositive appears at the end.)

   The final gift—hope—lay at the bottom of Pandora's box.

8. (Combine the two sentences below by turning the second sentence into an appositive. Repeat the word laws and place the appositive at the end of the sentence.)

Folks are pressing for new laws designed to restrict hunting. These are laws that have nothing to do with game protection or safety.

9. (Combine the sentences below by turning the first sentence into a negative appositive.)

   Merdine was never a threat to anyone.

   Merdine talked tough and walked with a swagger.

10. (Combine the two sentences below by turning the second sentence into an appositive.)

    Madge and I strolled through the graveyard.

    The graveyard is the most peaceful spot in town.

11. (Combine the following sentences into one clear sentence: turn the first three sentences into a list appositive.

    Jackie Robinson was a fierce competitor.
    Jackie Robinson was a daring runner.
    Jackie Robinson was a solid hitter.
    Jackie Robinson led the Brooklyn Dodgers to six World Series in his ten years with the team.

12. (Combine the following sentences into one clear sentence: turn sentences two through seven into an appositive.

    It was the kind of home that gathers memories like dust.

    It was a place filled with laughter.
    It was a place filled with play.
    It was a place filled with pain.
    It was a place filled with hurt.
    It was a place filled with ghosts.

It was a place filled with games.
It was a place filled with games.

Answers

In most cases, more than one combination is possible.

1. St. Valentine, the patron saint of lovers, was never married.
2. Lewis Carroll, a mathematics lecturer at Oxford University, is the author of Alice in Wonderland.
3. Willie Sarkis, a concert pianist in his youth, now plays for tips and drunks at the Rainbow Grill.
4. Pan, the pastoral god of fertility, is commonly depicted as a man with goat's horns, ears, and legs.
5. A sneaky, sinister man, Mr. Bun lingers in the alleys at dawn and creeps along the front walk every evening.
6. The filth in the air over Hawaii—an island far distant from the major sources of pollution—has increased dramatically over the past 30 years.
7. The final gift lay at the bottom of Pandora's box—hope.
8. Folks are pressing for new laws designed to restrict hunting—laws that have nothing to do with game protection or safety.
9. Never a threat to anyone, Merdine talked tough and walked with a swagger.
10. Madge and I strolled through the graveyard, the most peaceful spot in town.

11. A fierce competitor, a daring runner, and a solid hitter, Jackie Robinson led the Brooklyn Dodgers to six World Series in his ten years with the team.
12. It was the kind of home that gathers memories like dust—a place filled with laughter and play, pain and hurt, ghosts and games.

5

Absolute Phrase

An absolute phrase, or a nominative absolute, is generally —but not always—a group of words consisting of a noun/ pronoun and a participle as well as any related modifiers.

It is one more helpful linking device. For example, "His voice was trembling and his eyes were roving" and "He started to speak" can be joined as " His voice trembling and his eyes roving, he started to speak", where "His voice trembling and his eyes roving" – is an absolute phrase. The absolute phrase modifies the whole sentence rather than a particular word. It adds up new details to the general meaning of the sentence. Absolute phrases are regarded as parentheses and they are separated from the rest of the sentence either with a comma (pair of commas), or a dash (pair of dashes).

If the participle of an absolute phrase is expressed by the verb to be (e.g. being, having been), it is often omitted, but can be easily understood.

Examples: The party (being) in full swing, she decided to leave.

(Having been) married for twenty years, they could not imagine their lives without each other.

IDENTIFYING ABSOLUTE PHRASES

An absolute phrase is a word group that modifies an entire sentence. It consists of a noun plus at least one other word, as shown here:

The hunters rested for a moment in front of the shack, their breaths white in the frosty air.

The noun (*breaths*) that begins this absolute phrase is followed by an adjective (*white*) and a prepositional phrase (*in the frosty air*).

In addition to adjectives and prepositional phrases, adverbs and participles can also follow the noun in an absolute phrase. As the sentence above shows, an absolute phrase lets us move from a description of a *whole* person, place, or thing to just one or more parts: from *hunters*, for instance, to *their breaths*.

BUILDING AND ARRANGING ABSOLUTE PHRASES

Consider how the sentence just seen might be brokn down into two sentences:

— The hunters rested for a moment in front of the shack.

— Their breaths were white in the frosty air.

The second sentence, we see, can be turned into an absolute phrase simply by omitting the linking verb *were*. As we have seen, the absolute phrase may appear at the end of a sentence:

— The hunters rested for a moment in front of the shack, their breaths white in the frosty air.

The absolute phrase may also appear at the beginning of the sentence:

— Their breaths white in the frosty air, the hunters rested for a moment in front of the shack.

And occasionally an absolute phrase is positioned between the subject and verb:

— The hunters, their breaths white in the frosty air, rested for a moment in front of the shack.

Notice that an absolute phrase, like a participle phrase, is usually set off from the rest of the sentence by a pair of commas.

REVISING SENTENCES WITH ABSOLUTE PHRASES

As seen in Building Sentences with Absolute Phrases, these constructions are useful for adding details to an entire sentence—details that often describe one aspect of someone or something mentioned elsewhere in the sentence. Here we will practice revising sentences with absolute phrases.

Rewrite each sentence or set of sentences below according to the instructions in parentheses. When you are done, compare your revised sentences with those at the bottom of this page. Keep in mind that more than one correct response is possible.

1. (Combine the two sentences below: turn the second sentence into an absolute phrase and place it in front of the first sentence.)

   — The storks circled above us.

   — Their slender bodies were sleek and black against the orange sky.

2. {Combine the two sentences below: turn the second sentence into an absolute phrase and place it after the first sentence.)
   — On the tops of the hills, the grass stands at its tallest and greenest.
   — Its new seed plumes rise through a dead crop of last year's withered spears.
3. (Create two absolute phrases by eliminating the words in bold.)
   — Odysseus comes to shore, and the skin is torn from his hands, and the sea water is gushing from his mouth and nostrils.
4. (Combine the three sentences below: turn the second and third sentences into absolute phrases, and position them at the start of the sentence to establish a clear cause-effect relationship.))
   — Norton vowed never to marry again.
   — His first marriage ended in divorce.
   — His second marriage ended in despair.
5. (Omit when, and turn the main clause—in bold—into an absolute phrase.)
   — When the double giant Ferris wheel circles, the swaying seats are more frightening than a jet plane flying through a monsoon.
6. (Combine the following four sentences into a single sentence with a present participle phrase and two absolute phrases.)
   — All afternoon the caravan passed by.
   — The caravan shimmered in the winter light.

— Its numberless facets were gleaming.

— The hundreds of wagon wheels were turning in the dust in slow and endless motion.

7. (Combine the following five sentences into a single sentence with a present participle phrase and three absolute phrases.)

   — Six boys came over the hill.

   — The boys were running hard.

   — Their heads were down.

   — Their forearms were working.

   — Their breaths were whistling.

8. (Begin your new sentence with "The buildings sit empty," and turn the rest of the sentence into an absolute phrase.)

   — Jagged pieces of glass stick out of the frames of the hundreds of broken windows in the buildings that sit empty.

9. (Combine these sentences by replacing the period with a comma and eliminating the word in bold.)

   — Proud of my freedom and bumhood, I stood in the doorway of the boxcar, rocking with the motion of the train.

   — My ears were full of the rushing wind and the clattering wheels.

10. (Combine these three sentences by turning the first sentence into an absolute phrase and the third into a subordinate clause beginning with "where.")

— His hair was wet from the showers.

— He walked in the icy air to Luke's Luncheonette.

— There he ate three hamburgers in a booth with three juniors.

Answers:

1. Their slender bodies sleek and black against the orange sky, the storks circled above us.
2. On the tops of the hills, the grass stands at its tallest and greenest, its new seed plumes rising through a dead crop of last year's withered spears.
3. Odysseus comes to shore, the skin torn from his hands, the sea water gushing from his mouth and nostrils.
4. His first marriage having ended in divorce and his second in despair, Norton vowed never to marry again.
5. The double giant Ferris wheel circles, the swaying seats more frightening than a jet plane flying through a monsoon.
6. All afternoon the caravan passed by, shimmering in the winter light, its numberless facets gleaming and the hundreds of wagon wheels turning in the dust in slow and endless motion.
7. Six boys came over the hill, running hard, their heads down, their forearms working, their breaths whistling.

8. The buildings sit empty, jagged pieces of glass sticking out of the frames of the hundreds of broken windows.
9. Proud of my freedom and bumhood, I stood in the doorway of the boxcar, rocking with the motion of the train, my ears full of the rushing wind and the clattering wheels.
10. His hair wet from the showers, he walked in the icy air to Luke's Luncheonette, where he ate three hamburgers in a booth with three juniors.

6

American Idioms

SMELL A RAT

How come the front door is open? Didn't you close it before we went shopping?

I'm sure I did. I can't understand it. Frankly, I *smell a rat.*

Me, too. I'm *convinced that something is definitely wrong* here We'd better call the police.

GO TO THE DOGS

Have you seen their house lately? It's really *gone to the dogs.*

It's true that it has *become run-down and in serious need of repair,* but I'm sure that it can be fixed up to look like new.

I guess with a little carpentry work and some paint it could look pretty decent.

FISHY

When the security guard saw a light in the store after closing hours, it seemed to him that there was something *fishy* going on. He called the central office and explained to his superior that he thought something *strange and suspicious* was occurring.

TAKE THE BULL BY THE HORNS

Julie had always felt that she was missing out on a lot of fun because of her clumsiness on the dance floor. She had been putting off taking lessons, but she finally *took the bull by the horns* and went to a professional dance studio for help. She was tired of feeling left out and *acted decisively to correct the situation.*

LET THE CAT OUT OF THE BAG

Bob was going to retire from teaching in June, and the foreign language department was planning on presenting him with some luggage at his retirement dinner. He wasn't supposed to know about it, but someone *let the cat out of the bag*. At the dinner Bob acted surprised, even though someone *had told him what he was getting before the official presentation.*

FOR THE BIRDS

They went to a poetry reading, but they got bored and restless. As far as they were concerned, it was *for the birds*! They left during an intermission because they found the reading *totally uninteresting and meaningless*

STRAIGHT FROM THE HORSE'S MOUTH

How did you find out that Jill was engaged?

I got the information *from a very reliable source.*

You mean Jill told you so herself?

That's right. I got it *straight from the horse's mouth*!

HORSE AROUND

Did you hear about Dave's back injury?

No. How did he get hurt?

Well, after the coach left the gym he decided to stay and *horse around* on the parallel bars. He somehow lost his grip and fell on his back.

That's too bad, but he shouldn't have been *aimlessly playing around* on the equipment without proper supervision.

CAT GOT YOUR TONGUE?

Come on, Connie! Tell us what you think about our little ride down the rapids yesterday.

Well, uh...

Wasn't it exciting?

I, uh...

What's the matter? *Cat got your tongue*?

If you must know, I'm *keeping quiet* because I was scared out of my wits!

GET IN SOMEONE'S HAIR

Children! Would you please stop making so much noise!

And for heaven's sake, pick up your clothes and toys!

It's hard enough trying to keep this house clean without your throwing your things all over the place!

Clara, I know that the children *get in your hair,* but you should try not to let it upset you so much.

Listen, Jim. I can't help it . The children *bother me and make me very angry* when they're so noisy and messy.

SHOOT OFF ONE'S MOUTH

Jim doesn't play tennis very much, but he's always *shooting off his mouth* about how good he is. Yet he's fooling nobody. Jim is somewhat of a braggart and everyone knows that he gives opinions without knowing all the facts and *talks as if he knew everything about the game.*

JUMP DOWN SOMEONE'S THROAT

That's it, Greg! You'd better not come in after midnight again tonight!

I know, dad. You don't have to *jump down my throat*! I told you that I'd make it home around 11:30. I don't intend to be late!

Well, you've said that before and in you come at 2: 30 in the morning. You can't blame me for *getting angry and scolding you.* I've got good reason.

PAY THROUGH THE NOSE

At last Mr. Smith came upon the rare stamp he had been seeking at an auction. Since many other stamp collectors would also be bidding for it, he realised that he would have to *pay through the nose* in order to have it.

After considering the increasing value of the stamp, he decided that he would not mind *paying such a high price* for something so rare.

TONGUE-IN-CHEEK

Why were you teasing Sonia about her new hairdo? She really took offense at what you said.

I didn't mean to offend her. I was simply making a *tongue-in-cheek* remark when i said that it was too elaborate for a girl of her young, tender age.

Well, she thought you were serious. She had no idea that you were just saying that *as a joke*.

I'm really sorry. I suppose I owe her an apology.

PULL SOMEONE'S LEG

Hey, Al. I was invited to be a judge for the Miss America Beauty Pageant!

Oh, really? Come on, you're *pulling my leg*!

No, honestly. Do you really think that I'm trying to *fool you with a ridiculous story*?

Well, you've told me foolish stories before.

I can assure you that this one is for real.

PLAY IT BY EAR

Let's go to the movies, agreed?

Sure. And what'll we do after that ?

Oh, I don't know. Let's *play it by ear*.

Well, I would like to have a more definite plan of action.

Don't be like that. It's always more fun *not knowing what to expect and deciding what to do as we go along.*

STICK OUT ONE'S NECK

How come they're asking me to act as their guide through the jungle?

Evidently they think you're the only one who can lead them to the lost temple.

That jungle has danger lurking around every corner.

Why should I *stick my neck out* for them? They didn't pay me for my services.

They know that you would be *taking a great risk and could possibly get hurt,* but you're the only one with enough knowledge to take them to their destination. I'm sure you'll be amply rewarded.

ALL THUMBS

Hey Bea. Can you help me out ? I don't seem to be able to button up the back of my dress.

Sure. Let's see if I can do it for you.

I guess I'm *all thumbs* because I'm so nervous. I'm already late for my date.

Well, I suppose that being so nervous would make you *clumsy and awkward*. But don't worry. I'm sure your date will wait.

NOT HAVE A LEG TO STAND ON

Tom maintains that the firm owes him some back wages for having worked overtime. However, he *won't have a leg to stand on* unless he can prove that he put in all those extra hours. He doesn't stand a chance of getting his money *without a strong foundation of facts to support his position.*

GET OFF SOMEONE'S BACK

Hey, John. I'm bored. Come on, let's go out and do something.

Sorry, I'm right in the middle of studying for a physics exam. I won't be able to make it tonight.

You've been studying for a long time. Why don't you take a break ? Come on! Let's go ! Forget studying for a while !

Look! *Get off my back*! I can't go anywhere!

OK. I'll *stop bothering you* only if you promise to let me know the minute you're finished.

DRIVE SOMEONE UP A WALL

Wow ! What a great set of drums!

Yeah, they're great, but I can't play on them when my folks are at home. They say *I drive them up a wall* with all the loud banging.

I get the same thing at home. My folks tell me that I *annoy them and get them really angry* whenever I turn up the volume on my stereo.

STRING SOMEONE ALONG

Liz had high hopes of marrying Dean. When he ran

off with another woman, she realised that he was just *stringing her along*. She had felt very strongly about him and was really hurt to see that he was *deceiving her* and had no intentions of ever marrying her.

LEAVE SOMEONE HIGH AND DRY

Say, Jill. I thought that John was going to help you do the dishes tonight.

So did I. But he *left me high and dry*.

Where did he go ?

Well, he got a call from some of his pals at work to go bowling, and he *left me alone to do all this work without any help at all!*

SPILL THE BEANS

Did you know that Harry was going to take Kathy on a Caribbean cruise ?

Yes, I did. He was planning on surprising her with the tickets fro their anniversary, but someone *spilled the beans*.

What a shame ! That was supposed to have been a surprise.

Yes, it's too bad that someone *told her about the trip beforehand* and ruined Harry's surprise.

That's OK. Her enthusiasm was not dampened in the least!

BITE THE DUST

Andy did exceptionally well in all of the track events, but he *bit the dust* in the high jump competition. Much to the disappointment of his fans, he *went down in defeat, losing to a competitor* from the visiting team.

BEND OVER BACKWARDS

When Joan first started teaching she was afraid that she would have a lot of trouble getting used to the kids and to the faculty. Her fears turned out to be unfounded, since everybody *bent over backwards* to help her. Everyone *tried very hard* to help her feel comfortable and adjust to the school.

COUGH UP

Say, Greg. Did you finally get that computer that you wanted so much ?

Not yet. I needed to raise a couple of hundred dollars more.

Is it going to take you a while to raise the money?

It would have taken me forever, but dad said he'd *cough up* the money I need since I'm going to be using the computer for my school work.

Maybe it was *difficult for your dad to give* you the money but then, he knows that it's for a good cause.

JUMP THE GUN

Denise was planning on telling her grandparents that the doctor said she was going to have twins, but when her dad found out he *jumped the gun* and told them before Denise could say a word. He was so excited that he *became hasty* and revealed the news before Denise had a chance to tell them.

SCRATCH SOMEONE'S BACK

Hey, Bea. I need some help stacking these boxes. Would you please give me a hand?

OK. And I need some help tidying up the house. How about your helping me out after that ?

OK. If you *scratch my back, I'll scratch yours.*

I know you don't like doing housework, but I'll *help you with the boxes if you promise to return the favor.*

No problem. I'll even do the windows.

TURN SOMEONE OFF

How was your date with Marty last night ?

Well, it started of OK, but he really *turned me off* when we went for a snack after the movies.

Did he say or do something to annoy you?

Frankly, he *disgusted me* when he tried to talk with his mouth full.

I don't blame you . That would have really bothered me too.

KICK THE BUCKET

It's been said that the old man knew of a buried treasure, but he *kicked the bucket* before telling anyone where it was. If the treasure exists, the old man unfortunately took the secret of its location with him when he *died.*

WET BLANKET

James was not invited to go on the outing with the rest of the group because he's such a *wet blanket.* On many previous occasions he has *kept others from enjoying themselves by his pessimism and lack of enthusiasm.* It's understandable that no one wants him around.

UP ONE'S SLEEVE

All right, Sara. We know that you're planning something big for Jean's birthday. Mind telling us just what you have *up your sleeve* ?

I wanted to make his birthday a very special event.

Jean has a sister living in France, and I sent her an airplane ticket so that she could be here for his birthday.

Boy! That is something special. We kind of guessed that you had some *concealed plan* and were waiting for the right time to reveal it.

Well, I didn't want to say anything until I was sure she could come.

KNOCK SOMEONE'S SOCKS OFF

Hi, John. What's new ?

Oh, nothing too much with me, but you ought to see Fredo's new car. It'll *knock your socks off*!

So, he finally got that Italian sports car he's been dreaming about.

He sure did. When you see all the custom features that it has, you'll *get so enthused and excited* you won't know what to do.

Boy, I can hardly wait to go for a ride in it.

LOSE ONE'S SHIRT

I happened to bump into Dole at lunch yesterday afternoon.

What's new with Dole these days ?

He wasn't doing so well. For one thing, he told me he *lost his shirt* at the races.

Dole has always liked to bet on the horses. I'm not surprised that he *lost a great deal of money.*

Yeah. At this rate he'll never have a penny to his name.

LEMON

Have you seen Joe's new car yet ?

Yeah. It looks good, but she's had nothing but problems with it.

That's too bad. It sounds like she got a real *lemon*.

She sure did. No sooner did she drive it home from the dealer's than it proved *defective* and started breaking down.

OUT OF THE WOODS

Although Eric was well on his way to recovering from his bout with pneumonia, he was still not *out of the woods*. The doctors told him that he would have to take it easy and avoid exposure to cold, since he was not *out of danger and difficulty yet.*

EATING SOMEONE

Hey, Alice. What's been *eating you* lately ? Don't you realise how rude and irritable you've become?

I know. I'm really sorry for the way I've been acting.

Well, why don't you tell me what has been *bothering and upsetting you* and maybe we can work your problem out together.

I'll admit that it would help to talk to someone about it.

ON THE LINE

Lately Tom's been more conscientious about the accuracy and quality of his work with the company. He was warned that his job was *on the line* because of his lack of concern for his duties. When Tom was alerted that he was *in danger of losing his job,* he began to take his obligations with the company more seriously.

FEEL LIKE A MILLION DOLLARS

I bumped into Nick at the salon yesterday. He looked great, but I noticed that he had a slight limp when he walked.

I guess you didn't know that he had an operation on his knee.

No, I didn't. How's he feeling ?

He says he's *feeling like a million dollars* now. Apparently the pain in his knee is all gone.

It's good that he's *feeling so wonderful*. It must be a refreshing change not having to put up with all that discomfort.

HANG ON

During the depression years the Smiths had a great deal of trouble with their business, but somehow or other they were able to *hang on*. Although they almost lost their store, they managed to *persevere* until things got better.

MAKE ENDS MEET

It's almost impossible trying to keep up with the high cost of living.

It's true. Things are so expensive nowadays that it's very difficult to make ends meet.

You know, even with Lucie's salary, our combined income is *hardly enough to pay all the bills.*

MONEY TALKS

We've been waiting for three months to get delivery on our car, and people who put in their order after us have already gotten theirs.

Well, *money talks*. Why don't you try giving the dealer a little something extra to move things along?

I know full well that *money has the power to influence people*, but I refuse to pay extra for a service that is owed to me as a client.

If you want to have your car maybe you'd better reconsider.

7

Absolute Phrase

An absolute phrase, or a nominative absolute, is generally —but not always—a group of words consisting of a noun/ pronoun and a participle as well as any related modifiers.

It is one more helpful linking device. For example, "His voice was trembling and his eyes were roving" and "He started to speak" can be joined as " His voice trembling and his eyes roving, he started to speak", where "His voice trembling and his eyes roving" – is an absolute phrase. The absolute phrase modifies the whole sentence rather than a particular word. It adds up new details to the general meaning of the sentence. Absolute phrases are regarded as parentheses and they are separated from the rest of the sentence either with a comma (pair of commas), or a dash (pair of dashes).

If the participle of an absolute phrase is expressed by the verb to be (e.g. being, having been), it is often omitted, but can be easily understood.

Examples: The party (being) in full swing, she decided to leave.

(Having been) married for twenty years, they could not imagine their lives without each other.

IDENTIFYING ABSOLUTE PHRASES

An absolute phrase is a word group that modifies an entire sentence. It consists of a noun plus at least one other word, as shown here:

The hunters rested for a moment in front of the shack, *their breaths white in the frosty air.*

The noun (*breaths*) that begins this absolute phrase is followed by an adjective (*white*) and a prepositional phrase (*in the frosty air*).

In addition to adjectives and prepositional phrases, adverbs and participles can also follow the noun in an absolute phrase. As the sentence above shows, an absolute phrase lets us move from a description of a *whole* person, place, or thing to just one or more parts: from *hunters,* for instance, to *their breaths.*

BUILDING AND ARRANGING ABSOLUTE PHRASES

Consider how the sentence just seen might be brokn down into two sentences:

The hunters rested for a moment in front of the shack.Their breaths were white in the frosty air.

The second sentence, we see, can be turned into an absolute phrase simply by omitting the linking verb *were.* As we have seen, the absolute phrase may appear at the end of a sentence:

The hunters rested for a moment in front of the shack, their breaths white in the frosty air.

The absolute phrase may also appear at the beginning of the sentence:

Their breaths white in the frosty air, the hunters rested for a moment in front of the shack.

And occasionally an absolute phrase is positioned between the subject and verb:

The hunters, their breaths white in the frosty air, rested for a moment in front of the shack.

Notice that an absolute phrase, like a participle phrase, is usually set off from the rest of the sentence by a pair of commas.

REVISING SENTENCES WITH ABSOLUTE PHRASES

Here we will practice revising sentences with absolute phrases.

Exercises:

Rewrite each sentence or set of sentences below according to the instructions in parentheses. When you are done, compare your revised sentences with those at the bottom of this page. Keep in mind that more than one correct response is possible.

1. (Combine the two sentences below: turn the second sentence into an absolute phrase and place it in front of the first sentence.)
   - The storks circled above us.
   - Their slender bodies were sleek and black against the orange sky.
2. (Combine the two sentences below: turn the second sentence into an absolute phrase and place it after the first sentence.)

- On the tops of the hills, the grass stands at its tallest and greenest.
- Its new seed plumes rise through a dead crop of last year's withered spears.

3. (*Create two absolute phrases by eliminating the words in* ***bold***.)
   - Odysseus comes to shore, **and** the skin **is** torn from his hands, **and** the sea water **is** gushing from his mouth and nostrils.
4. (*Combine the three sentences below: turn the second and third sentences into absolute phrases, and position them at the start of the sentence to establish a clear cause-effect relationship.*))
   - Norton vowed never to marry again.
   - His first marriage ended in divorce.
   - His second marriage ended in despair.
5. (*Omit* ***when****, and turn the main clause—in bold—into an absolute phrase.*)
   - When the double giant Ferris wheel circles, the swaying seats are more frightening than a jet plane flying through a monsoon.
6. (Combine the following four sentences into a single sentence with a present participle phrase and two absolute phrases.) .
   - All afternoon the caravan passed by.
   - The caravan shimmered in the winter light.
   - Its numberless facets were gleaming.
   - The hundreds of wagon wheels were turning in the dust in slow and endless motion.

7. (*Combine the following five sentences into a single sentence with a present participle phrase and three absolute phrases.*)
   - Six boys came over the hill.
   - The boys were running hard.
   - Their heads were down.
   - Their forearms were working.
   - Their breaths were whistling.
8. (Begin your new sentence with "The buildings sit empty," and turn the rest of the sentence into an absolute phrase.)
   - Jagged pieces of glass stick out of the frames of the hundreds of broken windows in the buildings that sit empty.
9. (Combine these sentences by replacing the period with a comma and eliminating the word in bold.)
   - Proud of my freedom and bumhood, I stood in the doorway of the boxcar, rocking with the motion of the train.
   - My ears were full of the rushing wind and the clattering wheels.
10. (Combine these three sentences by turning the first sentence into an absolute phrase and the third into a subordinate clause beginning with "where.")
    - His hair was wet from the showers.
    - He walked in the icy air to Luke's Luncheonette.

– There he ate three hamburgers in a booth with three juniors.

Answers

1. Their slender bodies sleek and black against the orange sky, the storks circled above us.
2. On the tops of the hills, the grass stands at its tallest and greenest, its new seed plumes rising through a dead crop of last year's withered spears.
3. Odysseus comes to shore, the skin torn from his hands, the sea water gushing from his mouth and nostrils.
4. His first marriage having ended in divorce and his second in despair, Norton vowed never to marry again.
5. The double giant Ferris wheel circles, the swaying seats more frightening than a jet plane flying through a monsoon.
6. All afternoon the caravan passed by, shimmering in the winter light, its numberless facets gleaming and the hundreds of wagon wheels turning in the dust in slow and endless motion.
7. Six boys came over the hill, running hard, their heads down, their forearms working, their breaths whistling.
8. The buildings sit empty, jagged pieces of glass sticking out of the frames of the hundreds of broken windows.

9. Proud of my freedom and bumhood, I stood in the doorway of the boxcar, rocking with the motion of the train, my ears full of the rushing wind and the clattering wheels.
10. His hair wet from the showers, he walked in the icy air to Luke's Luncheonette, where he ate three hamburgers in a booth with three juniors.

8

Commonly Used Idioms

A

A bit much: If something is excessive or annoying, it is a bit much.

A chain is no stronger than its weakest link: This means that processes, organisations, etc, are vulnerable because the weakest person or part can always damage or break them.

A little learning is a dangerous thing: A small amount of knowledge can cause people to think they are more expert than they really are.eg. he said he'd done a course on home electrics, but when he tried to mend my table lamp, he fused all the lights! I think a little learning is a dangerous thing

A long row to hoe: Something that is a long row to hoe is a difficult task that takes a long time.

A lost ball in the high weeds: A lost ball in the high weeds is someone who does not know what they are doing, where they are or how to do something.

A penny for your thoughts: This idiom is used as a way of asking someone what they are thinking about.

A penny saved is a penny earned: This means that we shouldn't spend or waste money, but try to save it.

A picture is worth a thousand words: A picture can often get a message across much better than the best verbal description.

A poor man's something: Something or someone that can be compared to something or someone else, but is not as good is a poor man's version; a writer who uses lots of puns but isn't very funny would be a poor man's Oscar Wilde.

A watched pot never boils: Some things work out in their own time, so being impatient and constantly checking will just make things seem longer.

Abide by a decision: If you abide by a decision, you accept it and comply with it, even though you might disagree with it.

Abject lesson: (India) An abject lesson serves as a warning to others.

About as useful as a chocolate teapot: Someone or something that is of no practical use is about as useful as a chocolate teapot.

About face: If someone changes their mind completely, this is an about face. It can be used when companies, governments, etc, change their position on an issue.

Ace up your sleeve: If you have an ace up your sleeve, you have something that will give you an advantage that other people don't know about.

Achilles' heel: A person's weak spot is their Achilles' heel.

Acid test: An acid test is something that proves whether something is good, effective, etc, or not.

Across the board: If something applies to everybody, it applies across the board.

Add insult to injury: When people add insult to injury, they make a bad situation even worse.

After your own heart: A person after your own heart thinks the same way as you.

Against the clock: If you do something against the clock, you are rushed and have very little time to do it.

Against the grain: If doing something goes against the grain, you're unwilling to do it because it contradicts what you believe in, but you have no real choice.

Age before beauty: When this idiom is used, it is a way of allowing an older person to do something first, though often in a slightly sarcastic way.

Agony aunt: An agony aunt is a newspaper columnist who gives advice to people having problems, especially personal ones.

Alive and kicking: If something is active and doing well, it is alive and kicking.

All along: If you have known or suspected something all along, then you have felt this from the beginning.

All and sundry: This idiom is a way of emphasising 'all', like saying 'each and every one'.

All bark and no bite: Someone who talks a lot, but does nothing to back up their words— like a dog that barks at strangers, but won't actually bite.

All dressed up and nowhere to go: You're prepared for something that isn't going to happen.

All ears: If someone says they're all ears, they are very interested in hearing about something.

All eyes on me: If all eyes are on someone, then everyone is paying attention to them.

All fingers and thumbs: If you're all fingers and thumbs, you are too excited or clumsy to do something properly that requires manual dexterity. 'All thumbs' is an alternative form of the idiom.

All heart: Someone who is all heart is very kind and generous.

All over the map: (USA) If something like a discussion is all over the map, it doesn't stick to the main topic and goes off on tangents.

All over the place: If something is completely disorganised or confused, it is all over the place.

All over the shop: If something is completely disorganised or confused, it is all over the shop.

All over the show: If something is all over the show, it's in a complete mess.An alternative to 'All over the shop'.

Always a bridesmaid, never a bride: If someone is always a bridesmaid, never a bride, they never manage to fulfill their ambition- they get close, but never manage the recognition, etc, they crave.

Ambulance chaser: A lawyer who encourages people who have been in accidents or become ill to sue for compensation is an ambulance chaser.

Amen: Some use 'Amen' or 'Amen to that' as a way of agreeing with something that has just been said.

An apple a day keeps the doctor away: Eating healthy food keeps you healthy.

And all that jazz: This idiom means that everything related or similar is included.

Apron strings: A man who is tied to a woman's apron strings is excessively dependent on her, especially when it is his mother's apron strings.

Arm and a leg: If something costs an arm and a leg, it is very expensive.

Armchair critic: An armchair critic is someone who offers advice but never shows that they could actually do any better.

As one man: If people do something as one man, then they do it at exactly the same time or in complete agreement.

As the actress said to the bishop: (UK) This idiom is used to highlight a sexual reference, deliberate or accidental.

As the crow flies: This idiom is used to describe the shortest possible distance between two places.

As you sow, so shall you reap: This means that if you do bad things to people, bad things will happen to you, or good things if you do good things.

Asleep at the switch: If someone is asleep at the switch, they are not doing their job or taking their responsibilities very carefully. 'Asleep at the wheel' is an alternative.

Asleep at the wheel: If someone is asleep at the wheel, they are not doing their job or taking their responsibilities very carefully. 'Asleep at the switch' is an alternative.

At daggers drawn: If people are at daggers drawn, they are very angry and close to violence.

At death's door: If someone looks as if they are at death's door, they look seriously unwell and might actually be dying.

At each other's throats: If people are at each other's throats, they are fighting, arguing or competing ruthlessly.

At full tilt: If something is at full tilt, it is going or happening as fast or as hard as possible.

At large: If a criminal is at large, they have not been found or caught.

At loggerheads: If people are at loggerheads, they are arguing and can't agree on anything.

At loose ends: (USA) If you are at a loose end, you have spare time but don't know what to do with it.

At odds: If you are at odds with someone, you cannot agree with them and argue.

At sea: If things are at sea, or all at sea, they are disorganised and chaotic.

At the bottom of the totem pole: (USA) If someone is at the bottom of the totem pole, they are unimportant. Opposite is at the top of the totem pole.

At the coalface: If you work at the coalface, you deal with the real problems and issues, rather than sitting in a office discussing things in a detached way.

At the fore: In a leading position

At the top of my lungs: If you shout at the top of your lungs, you shout as loudly as you possibly can.

At the top of the list: If something is at the top of the list, it is of highest priority, most important, most urgent, or the next in one's line of attention.

At the top of your lungs: If you shout at the top of your lungs, you shout as loudly as you possibly can.

At the top of your voice: If you talk, shout or sing at the top of your voice, you do it as loudly as you can.

At your wit's end: If you're at your wit's end, you really don't know what you should do about something, no matter how hard you think about it.

At your wits' end: If you are at your wits' end, you have no idea what to do next and are very frustrated.

Average Joe: An average Joe is an ordinary person without anything exceptional about them.

Avowed intent: If someone makes a solemn or serious promise publicly to attempt to reach a certain goal, this is their avowed intent.

Away with the fairies: If someone is away with the fairies, they don't face reality and have unrealistic expectations of life.

Awe inspiring: Something or someone that is awe inspiring amazes people in a slightly frightening but positive way.

Axe to grind: If you have an axe to grind with someone or about something, you have a grievance, a resentment and you want to get revenge or sort it out. In American English, it is 'ax'.

B

Babe in arms: A babe in arms is a very young child, or a person who is very young to be holding a position.

Babe in the woods: A babe in the woods is a naive, defenceless, young person.

Baby boomer: (USA) A baby boomer is someone born in the years after the end of the Second World War, a period when the population was growing very fast.

Back burner: If an issue is on the back burner, it is being given low priority.

Back foot: (UK) If you are on your back foot, you are at a disadvantage and forced to be defensive of your position.

Back number: Something that's a back number is dated or out of fashion.

Back the wrong horse: If you back the wrong horse, you give your support to the losing side in something.

Back to back: If things happen back to back, they are directly one after another.

Back to square one: If you are back to square one, you have to start from the beginning again.

Back to the drawing board: If you have to go back to the drawing board, you have to go back to the beginning and start something again.

Back to the salt mine: If someone says they have to go back to the salt mine, they have to return to work.

Back to the wall: If you have your back to the wall, you are in a difficult situation with very little room for manoeuvre.

Backseat driver: A backseat driver is an annoying person who is fond of giving advice to the person performing a task or doing something, especially when the advice is either wrong or unwelcome.

Bag of bones: If someone is a bag of bones, they are very underweight.

Bag of nerves: If someone is a bag of nerves, they are very worried or nervous.

Ballpark figure: A ballpark figure is a rough or approximate number (guesstimate) to give a general idea of something, like a rough estimate for a cost, etc.

Banana republic: Banana republic is a term used for small countries that are dependent on a single crop or resource and governed badly by a corrupt elite.

Bandit territory: An area or an industry, profession, etc, where rules and laws are ignored or flouted is bandit territory.

Baptism of fire: A baptism of fire was a soldier's first experience of shooting. Any unpleasant experience undergone, usually where it is also a learning experience, is a baptism of fire.

Bar fly: A bar fly is a person who spends a lot of time drinking in different bars and pubs.

Bark is worse than their bite: Someone who's bark is worse than their bite may well get angry and shout, but doesn't take action.

Barking up the wrong tree: If you are barking up the wrong tree, it means that you have completely misunderstood something or are totally wrong.

Barkus is willing: This idiom means that someone is willing to get married.

Barrack-room lawyer: (UK) A barrack-room lawyer is a person who gives opinions on things they are not qualified to speak about.

Barrel of laughs: If someone's a barrel of laughs, they are always joking and you find them funny.

Basket case: If something is a basket case, it is so bad that it cannot be helped.

Bat an eyelid: If someone doesn't bat an eyelid, they don't react or show any emotion when surprised, shocked, etc.

Batten down the hatches: If you batten down the hatches, you prepare for the worst that could happen to you.

Be all ears: If you are all ears, you are very eager to hear what someone has to say.

Be careful what you wish for: If you get things that you desire, there may be unforeseen and unpleasant consequences.

Be on the pig's back: If you're on the pig's back, you're happy / content / in fine form.

Be out in force: If people are out in force, they are present somewhere in large numbers.

Beat about the bush: If someone doesn't say clearly what they mean and try to make it hard to understand, they are beating about (around) the bush.

Beauty is in the eye of the beholder: Beauty is in the eye of the beholder means that different people will find different things beautiful and that the differences of opinion don't matter greatly.

Beauty is only skin deep: This idiom means that appearances can be deceptive and something that seems or looks good may turn out to be bad.

Beck and call: Someone who does everything for you, no matter when you ask, is at your beck and call.

Bedroom eyes: Someone with bedroom eyes has a sexy look in their eyes.

Bee in your bonnet: If someone is very excited about something, they have a bee in their bonnet.

Bee's Knees: If something is the bee's knees, it's outstanding or the best in its class.

Beeline for: If you make a beeline for a place, you head there directly.

Been in the wars: (UK) If someone has been in the wars, they have been hurt or look as if they have been in a struggle.

Been there, done that: People say this when they have already experienced what is being discussed.

Before the ink is dry: If people make an agreement or contract and then the situation changes very quickly, it changes before the ink is dry.

Beg the question: In philosophy "to beg the question" is to assume something to be true that has not yet been proved. I have seen the idiom also to mean that a question is crying out to be asked.

Beggars can't be choosers: This idiom means that people who are in great need must accept any help that is offered, even if it is not a complete solution to their problems.

Behind closed doors: If something happens away from the public eye, it happens behind closed doors.

Believe in the hereafter: A belief in the hereafter is a belief in the afterlife, or life after death. It is, therefore, associated with religions and the soul's journey to heaven or to hell, whichever way being just deserts for the person based on how they led their life.

Below par: If something isn't up to standard, or someone isn't feeling or doing very well, they are below par.

Below the belt: If someone says something that is cruel or unfair, it is below the belt, like the illegal punches in boxing.

Bend someone's ear: To bend someone's ear is to talk to someone about something for a long-enough period that it becomes tiresome for the listener.

Benjamin of the family: The Benjamin of the family is the youngest child.

Beside the point: If something is beside the point, it's not relevant to the matter being discussed or considered.

Beside themselves: If people are beside themselves, they are very worried or emotional about something.

Beside yourself: If you are beside yourself, you are extremely angry.

Best of a bad bunch: The best that could be obtained from a list of options that were not exactly what was required.

Best of both worlds: If you have the best of both worlds, you benefit from different things that do not normally go together.

Better half: Your better half is your husband or wife.

Better late than never: This idiom suggests that doing something late is better than not doing it at all.

Better safe than sorry: This idiom is used to recommend being cautious rather than taking a risk.

Better than a stick in the eye: If something is better than a stick in the eye, it isn't very good, but it is better than nothing.

Better the devil you know: This is the shortened form of the full idiom, 'better the devil you know than the devil you don't', and means that it is often better to deal with someone or something you are familiar with and know, even if they are not ideal, than take a risk with an unknown person or thing.

Between the devil and the deep blue sea: If you are caught between the devil and the deep blue sea, you are in a dilemma; a difficult choice.

Birds of a feather flock together: This idiom means that people with similar interests will stick together.

Birthday suit: If you are in your birthday suit, you are naked.

Bite someone's head off: If you bite someone's head off, you criticise them angrily.

Bite the bullet: If you have to bite the bullet, you have to accept or face something unpleasant because it cannot be avoided.

Bite the dust: This is a way of saying that somebody has died, especially if they are killed violently like a soldier in battle.

Bite your lip: If you have to bite your lip, you have to make a conscious effort not to react or to keep quiet about something that displeases you.

Bite your tongue: If you bite your tongue, you refrain from speaking because it is socially or otherwise better not to.

Bits and bobs: Bits and bobs are small, remnant articles and things- the same as 'odds and ends'.

Bitter end: If you do something to the bitter end, you do it to the very end, no matter how unsuccessful you are.

Bitter pill to swallow: A bitter pill to swallow is something that is hard to accept.

Black hole: If there is a black hole in financial accounts, money has disappeared.

Black sheep: Someone who is the black sheep doesn't fit into a group or family because their behaviour or character is not good enough.

Blackball: If you vote against allowing someone to be a member of an organisation or group, you are blackballing him or her.

Blessing in disguise: If some bad luck or misfortune ultimately results in something positive, it's a blessing in disguise.

Blind as a bat: If you are in total darkness and can't see anything at all, you are as blind as a bat.

Blind leading the blind: When the blind are leading the blind, the people in charge of something don't know anything more than the people they are in charge of, when they should have greater knowledge.

Blood from a turnip: It is impossible to get something from someone if they don't have it, just as you cannot get blood from a turnip.

Blood is thicker than water: This idiom means that family relationships are stronger than others.

Blow out of the water: If something, like an idea, is blown out of the water, it is destroyed or defeated comprehensively.

Blow the cobwebs away: If you blow the cobwebs away, you make sweeping changes to something to bring fresh views and ideas in.

Blow the whistle: If somebody blows the whistle on a plan, they report it to the authorities.

Blow your top: If someone blows their top, they lose their temper.

Blue blood: Someone with blue blood is royalty.

Blue-eyed boy: Someone's blue-eyed boy is their favourite person.

Body politic: A group of people organised under a single government or authority (national or regional) is a body politic.

Bold as brass: Someone who is as bold as brass is very confident and not worried about how other people will respond or about being caught.

Bolt from the blue: If something happens unexpectedly and suddenly, it is a bolt from the blue.

Bounce off the walls: If someone's bouncing off the walls, they are very excited about something.

Bouquet of orchids: Id someone deserves a bouquet of orchids, they have done something worthy of praise.

Box and dice: Box and dice means everything.

Boxing and coxing: If people are boxing and coxing, they are sharing responsibilities so that one of them is working while the other isn't. It can also be used when couples are sharing a house, but their relationship has broken down and when one is at home, the other stays out.

Boys in blue: The boys in blue are the police.

Brain surgery: If something is not brain surgery, it isn't very complicated or difficult to understand or master.

Brass monkey: If it's brass monkey weather, or cold enough to freeze the balls off a brass monkey, it is extremely cold.

Brass tacks: If you get down to brass tacks, you get down to the real business.

Bread and butter: Bread and butter issues are ones that affect people directly and in a very important way.

Breadwinner: Used to describe the person that earns the most money. For example - She's the breadwinner in the family.

Break a leg: This idiom is a way of wishing someone good luck.

Break even: If you break even, you don't make any money, but you don't lose any either.

Break ground: If you break ground, or break new ground, you make progress, taking things into a new area or going further than anyone has gone before. 'Ground-breaking' is used an adjective.

Break the back of the beast: If you break the back of the beast, you accomplish a challenge.

Break the ice: When you break the ice, you get over any initial embarrassment or shyness when you meet someone for the first time and start conversing.

Breathe your last: When you breathe your last, you die.

Bridge the gap: If you bridge the gap, you make a connection where there is a great difference.

Bright and breezy: When someone is cheerful and full of energy, they are bright and breezy.

Bright as a button: A person who is as bright as a button is very intelligent or smart.

Bright-eyed and bushy-tailed: If someone's bright-eyed and bushy-tailed, they are full of energy and enthusiasm.

Brighten up the day: If something brightens up your day, something happens that makes you feel positive and happy all day long.

Bring a knife to a gunfight: If someone brings a knife to a gunfight, they are very badly prepared for something.

Bring home the bacon: A person who brings home the bacon earns the money that a family live on.

Bring the house down: Something that brings the house down is acclaimed and praised vigorously.

Bring to the table: If you bring something to the table, you make a contribution or an offer in a discussion or negotiation..

Brown nose: When someone tries to make themselves popular with somebody, usually in a position of authority, especially by flattering them, they are brown nosing.

Bull market: A bull market is a period when investors are optimistic and there are expectations that good financial results will continue.

Bull session: If you have a bull session, you have an informal group discussion about something.

Bundle of nerves: Someone who is a bundle of nerves is very worried or nervous.

Burn rubber: If you burn rubber, you drive very fast to get somewhere.

Burn the candle at both ends: Someone who burns the candle at both ends lives life at a hectic pace, doing things which are likely to affect their health badly.

Burn the midnight oil: If you stay up very late working or studying, you burn the midnight oil.

Burn your bridges: If you burn your bridges, you do something that makes it impossible to go back from the position you have taken.

Burn your fingers: If you burn your fingers, you suffer a loss or something unpleasant as the result of something you did, making you less likely to do it again.

Burning question: A burning question is something we all want to know about.

Burst at the seams: To be filled to or beyond normal capacity: This room will be bursting at the seams when all the guests arrive.

Bury the hatchet: If you bury the hatchet, you make peace with someone and stop arguing or fighting.

Bury your head in the sand: If someone buries their head in the sand, they ignore something that is obviously wrong.

Busman's holiday: A busman's holiday is when you spend your free time doing the same sort of work as you do in your job.

Bust my chops: When someone says that they're not going to bust their chops, it means they are not going to work that hard or make much effort.

Busted flush: Someone or something that had great potential but ended up a useless failure is a busted flush.

Busy as a beaver: If you're as busy as a beaver, you're very busy indeed.

Busy as a bee: If you are as busy as a bee, you are very busy indeed.

Butt naked: If someone is butt naked, they have no clothes on at all, often when they can be seen.

Butt of a joke: If something or someone becomes the butt of a joke it or they are not taken seriously anymore.

Butter wouldn't melt in their mouth: If someone looks as if butter wouldn't melt in their mouth, they look very innocent.

Butterfingers: Someone who has butterfingers is clumsy and drops things.

Buy the farm: When somebody has bought the farm, they have died.

By a hair's breadth: If a person escapes from some danger by a hair's breadth, they only just managed to avoid it. The breadth is the thickness of a hair, so they probably feel somewhat lucky because the margin between success and what could easily have been failure was so close.

By a whisker: If you do something by a whisker, you only just manage to do it and come very near indeed to failing.

By and large: By and large means usually or generally.

By cracky: A term used by rural folks in years past to emphasize a matter of importance or urgency. An example: 'By cracky, you need to get out there in the field with that mule and plow and finish the sod-busting before dark.'

By dint of: This means 'as a result of' or 'because of': It would be good to think he'd risen to position of Chief Executive by dint of hard work.

By heart: If you learn something by heart, you learn it word for word.

By hook or by crook: If you are prepared to do something by hook or by crook, you are willing to do anything, good or bad, to reach your goal.

By leaps and bounds: Something that happens by leaps and bounds happens very quickly in big steps.

By the back door: If something is started or introduced by the back door, then it is not done openly or by following the proper procedures.

By the book: If you do something by the book, you do it exactly as you are supposed to.

By the numbers: If something is done by the numbers, it is done in a mechanical manner without room for creativity.

By the same token: If someone applies the same rule to different situations, they judge them by the same token: If things go well, he's full of praise, but, by the same token, when things go wrong he gets furious.

By the seat of your pants: If you do something by the seat of your pants, you do it without help from anyone.

By the skin of your teeth: If you do something by the skin of your teeth, you only just manage to do it and come very near indeed to failing.

By word of mouth: If something becomes known by word of mouth, it gets known by being talked about rather than through publicity or advertising, etc.

C

Cake's not worth the candle: If someone says that the cake's not worth the candle, they mean that the result will not be worth the effort put in to achieve it.

Calf lick: A calf lick is the weird parting in your fringe where your hair grows in a different direction, usually to one side.

Call a spade a spade: A person who calls a spade a spade is one speaks frankly and makes little or no attempt to conceal their opinions or to spare the feelings of their audience.

Call it a day: If you call it a day, you stop doing something for a while, normally at least until the following day.

Call on the carpet: If you are called on the carpet, you are summoned for a reprimand by superiors or others in power.

Calm before the storm: A calm time immediately before period of violent activity or argument is the calm before the storm.

Can of worms: If an action can create serious problems, it is opening a can of worms.

Can't do it for toffee: If you can't so something for toffee, you are incapable of doing something properly or to any sort of standard.

Can't hold a candle: If something can't hold a candle to something else, it is much worse.

Card up your sleeve: If you have a card up your sleeve, you have a surprise plan or idea that you are keeping back until the time is right.

Carpetbagger: A carpetbagger is an opportunist without any scruples or ethics, or a politican who wants to represent a place they have no connection with.

Carry the can: If you carry the can, you take the blame for something, even though you didn't do it or are only partly at fault.

Case by case: If things are done case by case, each situation or issue is handled separately on its own merits and demerits.

Cash in your chips: If you cash in your chips, you sell something to get what profit you can because you think its value is going to fall. It can also mean 'to die'.

Cast aspersion: If you cast aspersion, you try to blacken someone's name and make people think badly of them.

Cast doubt on: If you make other people not sure about a matter, then you have cast doubt on it.

Cast iron stomach: A person with a cast iron stomach can eat or drink anything without any ill effects.

Cast sheep's eyes at: If you cast sheep's eyes at at someone, you look lovingly or with longing at them.

Cast your mind back: If somebody tells you to cast your mind back on something, they want you to think about something that happened in the past, but which you might not remember very well, and to try to remember as much as possible.

Cast your net widely: If you cast your net widely, you use a wide range of sources when trying to find something.

Casting vote: The casting vote is a vote given to a chairman or president that is used when there is a deadlock.

Castles in the air: Plans that are impractical and will never work out are castles in the air.

Cat among the pigeons: If something or someone puts, or sets or lets, the cat among the pigeons, they create a disturbance and cause trouble.

Cat and dog life: If people lead a cat and dog life, they are always arguing.

Cat burglar: A cat burglar is a skillful thief who breaks into places without disturbing people or setting off alarms.

Cat nap: If you have a short sleep during the day, you are cat napping.

Cat's whiskers: Something excellent is the cat's whiskers.

Catch as catch can: This means that people should try to get something any way they can.

Catch some z's: If you catch some z's, you get some sleep.

Catch someone red-handed: If someone is caught red-handed, they are found doing something wrong or illegal.

Catch-22: Catch-22 is a situation where conflicting rules make the desired outcome impossible. It comes from a novel by the American author Joseph Heller, in which pilots would not have to fly missions if they were mentally ill, but not wanting to fly dangerous missions was held to be proof of sanity, so they had to fly anyway.

Chase rainbows: If someone chases rainbows, they try to do something that they will never achieve.

Chase your tail: If you are chasing your tail, you are very busy but not being very productive.

Cheek by jowl: If things or people are cheek by jowl, they are very close together.

Chinese whispers: (UK) When a story is told from person to person, especially if it is gossip or scandal, it inevitably gets distorted and exaggerated. This process is called Chinese whispers.

Chop and change: If things chop and change, they keep changing, often unexpectedly.

Cigarette paper: If you cannot get or put a cigarette paper between people, they are so closely bonded that nothing will separate them or their positions on issues.

Circle the wagons: (USA) If you circle the wagons, you stop communicating with people who don't think the same way as you to avoid their ideas. It can also mean to bring everyone together to defend a group against an attack.

Clean bill of health: If something or someone has a clean bill of health, then there's nothing wrong; everything's fine.

Close shave: If you have a close shave, you very nearly have a serious accident or get into trouble.

Close the stable door after the horse has bolted: If people try to fix something after the problem has occurred, they are trying to close the stable door after the horse has bolted. 'Close the barn door after the horse has bolted' is alternative, often used in American English.

Closed book to me: If a subject is a closed book to you, it is something that you don't understand or know anything about.

Cloth ears: If you don't listen to people, they may suggest you have cloth ears.

Cloud cuckoo land: If someone has ideas or plans that are completely unrealistic, they are living on cloud cuckoo land.

Cloud nine: If you are on cloud nine, you are extremely happy.

Cloud of suspicion: If a cloud of suspicion hangs over an individual, it means that they are not believed or are distrusted.

Cloud on the horizon: If you can see a problem ahead, you can call it a cloud on the horizon.

Clutch at straws: If someone is in serious trouble and tries anything to help them, even though their chances of success are probably nil, they are clutching at straws.

Clutch play: If an activity is referred to as a clutch play, it means that the activity was the key to the success or failure of the venture. For instance, a clutch play in a baseball game may be striking out a batter with the bases loaded.

Coast is clear: When the coast is clear, the people supposed to be watching you are not there and you are able to move or leave.

Cock a snook: To make a rude gesture by putting one thumb to the nose with the fingers outstretched.

Cock and bull story: A cock and bull story is a lie someone tells that is completely unbelievable.

Cock in the henhouse: This is used to describe a male in an all-female environment.

Cock of the walk: A man who is excessively confident and thinks he's better than other people is the cock of the walk.

Cold day in hell: This is used as a prediction there is no chance some event or condition will ever happen.'There will be a cold day in hell before he manages it.'

Cold feet: If you get cold feet about something, you lose the courage to do it.

Cold turkey: If someone suddenly stops taking drugs, instead of slowly cutting down, they do cold turkey.

Colder than a witches tit: If it is colder than a witches tit, it is extremely cold outside.

Collateral damage: Accidental or unintended damage or casualties are collateral damage.

Come clean: If someone comes clean about something, they admit to deceit or wrongdoing.

Come hell or high water: If someone says they'll do something come hell or high water, they mean that nothing will stop them, no matter what happens.

Come out in the wash: If something will come out in the wash, it won't have any permanent negative effect.

Come out of the woodwork: When things come out of the woodwork, they appear unexpectedly.

Come out of your shell: If someone comes out of their shell, they stop being shy and withdrawn and become more friendly and sociable.

Come rain or shine: If I say I'll be at a place come rain or shine, I mean that I can be relied on to turn up; nothing, not even the vagaries of British weather, will deter me or stop me from being there.

Come to a head: If events reach a crisis point, they come to a head.

Come to bear: If something comes to bear on you, you start to feel the pressure or effect of it.

Come to call: If someone comes to call, they respond to an order or summons directly.

Come to grips: If you come to grips with a problem or issue, you face up to it and deal with it.

Come to heel: If someone comes to heel, they stop behaving in a way that is annoying to someone in authority and start being obedient.

Come what may: If you're prepared to do something come what may, it means that nothing will stop or distract you, no matter how hard or difficult it becomes.

Come with the territory: If something comes with the territory, it is part of a job or responsibility and just has to be accepted, even if unpleasant.

Comes with the territory: If something comes with the territory, especially when undesirable, it is automatically included with something else, like a job, responsibility, etc.

Connect the dots: When you connect the dots, you understand the connections and relationships.

Constitution of an ox: If someone has the constitution of an ox, they are less affected than most people by things like tiredness, illness, alcohol, etc.

Cook up a storm: If someone cooks up a storm, they cause a big fuss or generate a lot of talk about something.

Cool as a cat: To act fine when you a actually scared or nervous

Cream of the crop: The cream of the crop is the best there is.

Cream rises to the top: A good person or idea cannot go unnoticed for long, just as cream poured in coffee or tea eventually rises to the top.

Cut to the chase: If you cut to the chase, you get to the point, or the most interesting or important part of something without delay.

Cut to the quick: If someone's cut to the quick by something, they are very hurt and upset indeed.

Cut your teeth on: The place where you gain your early experience is where you cut your teeth.

Cuts no ice: If something cuts no ice, it doesn't have any effect or influence.

Cutting edge: Something that is cutting edge is at the forefront of progress in its area.

D

Daft as a brush: (UK) Someone who is daft as a brush is rather stupid.

Damp squib: (UK) If something is expected to have a great effect or impact but doesn't, it is a damp squib.

Dancing on someone's grave: If you will dance on someone's grave, you will outlive or outlast them and will celebrate their demise.

Dark horse: If someone is a dark horse, they are a bit of a mystery.

Davey Jones' locker: Davey Jones' locker is the bottom of the sea or resting place of drowned sailors.

Day in the sun: If you have your day in the sun, you get attention and are appreciated.

Daylight robbery: If you are overcharged or underpaid, it is a daylight robbery; open, unfair and hard to prevent. Rip-off has a similar meaning.

Days are numbered: When someone's days are numbered, they are expected to die soon.

Dead air: When there is a period of total silence, there is dead air.

Dead and buried: If something is dead and buried, it has all long been settled and is not going to be reconsidered.

Dead as a dodo: If something's dead as a dodo, it is lifeless and dull. The dodo was a bird that lived the island of Mauritius. It couldn't fly and was hunted to extinction.

Dead as a doornail: This is used to indicate that something is lifeless.

Dead duck: if something is a dead duck, it is a failure.

Dead even: If people competing are dead even, they are at exactly the same stage or moving at exactly the same speed.

Dead from the neck up: Someone who's dead from the neck up is very stupid indeed.

Dead heat: If a race ends in a dead heat, two or more finish with exactly the same result.

Dead heat: If people finish a race or competition at axactly the same time and it is impossible to declare one of them the winner, it's a dead heat.

Dead in the water: If something is dead in the water, it isn't going anywhere or making any progress.

Dead level best: If you try your dead level best, you try as hard as you possibly could to do something.

Dead man walking: A dead man walking is someone who is in great trouble and will certainly get punished, lose their job or position, etc, soon.

Dead meat: This is used as a way of threatening someone: You'll be dead meat if you don't go along.

Dead men's shoes: If promotion or success requires replacing somebody, then it can only be reached by dead men's shoes' by getting rid of them.

Dear John letter: A letter written by a partner explaining why they are ending the relationship is a Dear John letter.

Death of a thousand cuts: If something is suffering the death of a thousand cuts, or death by a thousand cuts, lots of small bad things are happening, none of which are fatal in themselves, but which add up to a slow and painful demise.

Death warmed up: (UK) If someone looks like death warmed up, they look very ill indeed.

Decorate the mahogany: (USA) When someone buys a round a pub or bar, they decorate the mahogany; putting cash on the bar.

Deep pockets: If someone has deep pockets, they are wealthy.

Deep pockets but short arms: Someone who has money but never puts his hand in his pocket to pay for anything has deep pockets but short arms.

Deer in the headlights: When one is caught offguard and needs to make a decision, but cannot react quickly.

Deliver the goods: Do what is required, come up to expectations. For example, Kate delivered the goods and got us the five votes we needed. This phrase alludes to delivering an order of groceries or other items. [Colloquial; second half of 1800s]

Demon weed: Tobacco is the demon weed.

Derring-do: If a person shows derring-do, they show great courage.

Devil finds work for idle hands: When people say that the devil finds work for idle hands, they mean that if people don't have anything to do with their time, they are more likely to get involved in trouble and criminality.

Devil is in the detail: When people say that the devil in the detail, they mean that small things in plans and schemes that are often overlooked can cause serious problems later on.

Diamond in the rough: A diamond in the rough is someone or something that has great potential, but isn't not refined and polished.

Die is cast: If the die is cast, a decision has been made that cannot be altered and fate will decide the consequences.

Different kettle of fish: If something is a different kettle of fish, it is very different from the other things referenced.

Different ropes for different folks: (USA) This idiom means that different people do things in different ways that suit them.

Different strokes for different folks: (USA) This idiom means that different people do things in different ways that suit them.

Dig way down deep: When someone digs way down deep, they look into their inner feelings to see how they feel about it.

Dig your heels in: If you dig your heels in, you start to resist something.

Dime a dozen: (USA) If something is a dime a dozen, it is extremely common, possibly too common.

Dine on ashes: I someone is dining on ashes he or she is excessively focusing attention on failures or regrets for past actions.

Dinosaur: A dinosaur is a person who is thought to be too old for their position.

Dip your toes in the water: If you dip your toes in the water, you try something tentatively because you are not sure whether it will work or not.

Dirty dog: A dirty dog is an untrustworthy person.

Discerning eye: If a person has a discerning eye, they are particularly good at judging the quality of something.

Discretion is the better part of valour: This idiom means that it is often better to think carefully and not act than to do something that may cause problems.

Dish the dirt: If you dish the dirt on something or someone, you make unpleasant or shocking information public.

Do a Devon Loch: (UK) If someone does a Devon Loch, they fail when they were very close to winning. Devon Loch was a horse that collapsed just short of the winning line of the Grand National race.

Do a Lord Lucan: (UK) If someone disappears without a trace or runs off, they do a Lord Lucan.

Do a runner: (UK) If people leave a restaurant without paying, they do a runner.

Do as you would be done by: Treat and respect others as you would hope to be respected and treated by them.

Do the needful: (India) If you do the needful, you do what is necessary.

Do the running: (UK) The person who has to do the running has to make sure that things get done. ('Make the running' is also used.)

Do their dirty work: Someone who does someone's dirty work, carries out the unpleasant jobs that the first person doesn't want to do. Someone who seems to enjoy doing this is sometimes known as a 'henchman'.

Do's and don't's: The do's and don't's are what is acceptable or allowed or not within an area or issue, etc.

Dodge the bullet: If someone has dodged a bullet, they have successfully avoided a very serious problem.

Dog and pony show: (USA) A dog and pony show is a presentation or some marketing that has lots of style, but no real content.

Dog days: Dog days are very hot summer days.

Dog eat dog: In a dog eat dog world, there is intense competition and rivalry, where everybody thinks only of himself or herself.

Dog in the manger: (UK) If someone acts like a dog in the manger, they don't want other people to have or enjoy things that are useless to them.

Dog tired: If you are dog tired, you are exhausted.

Dog's dinner: Something that is a dog's dinner is a real mess.

Dog's life: If some has a dog's life, they have a very unfortunate and wretched life.

Dog-eared: If a book is dog-eared, it is in bad condition, with torn pages, etc.

Dog-whistle politics: (AU) When political parties have policies that will appeal to racists while not being overtly racist, they are indulging in dog-whistle politics.

Don't bite the hand that feeds: When someone says this to you, they are trying to tell you not to act against those on whom you depend.

Don't catch your chickens before they're hatched: This means that you should wait until you know whether something has produced the results you desire, rather than acting beforehand.

Don't cry over spilt milk: When something bad happens and nothing can be done to help it people say, 'Don't cry over spilt milk'.

Don't give up the day job: This idiom is used a way of telling something that they do something badly.

Don't hold your breath: If you are told not to hold your breath, it means that you shouldn't have high expectations about something.

Don't judge a book by the cover: This idiom means that you should not judge something or someone by appearances, but should look deeper at what is inside and more important.

Don't know whether to wind a watch or bark at the moon: If you don't know what to do, you don't know whether to wind a watch or bark at the moon.

Don't push my buttons!: This can be said to someone who is starting to annoy you.

Don't stand there with curlers in your hair: This means 'don't keep me waiting'. It's said to someone who is taking too long to get moving.

Don't throw bricks when you live in a glass house: Don't call others out on actions that you, yourself do. Don't be a hypocrite.

Don't trouble trouble until trouble troubles you: Don't go looking for trouble or problems- let them come to you.

Don't upset the applecart: If you are advised not to upset the applecart, you are being told not to disturb the way things are done because it might ruin things.

Don't wash your dirty laundry in public: (UK) People, especially couples, who argue in front of others or involve others in their personal problems and crises, are said to be washing their dirty laundry in public; making public things that are best left private.

Done to death: If a joke or story has been done to death, it has been told so often that it has stopped being funny.

Donkey's years: This idiom means 'a very long time'.

Double whammy: A double whammy is when something causes two problems at the same time, or when two setbacks occur at the same time.

Double-edged sword: If someone uses an argument that could both help them and harm them, then they are using a double-edged sword sword; it cuts both ways.

Doubting Thomas: A Doubting Thomas is someone who only believes what they see themselves, not what they are told.

Down and out: If someone is down and out, they are desperately poor and need help.

Down at heel: Someone who is down at heel is short of money.

Down for the count: If someone is down for the count, they have lost a struggle, like a boxer who has been knocked out.

Down in the doldrums: If somebody's down in the doldrums, they are depressed and lacking energy.

Down in the dumps: If someone's down in the dumps, they are depressed.

Down in the mouth: If someone is down in the mouth, they look unhappy or depressed.

Down the drain: If something goes down the drain, especially money or work, it is wasted or produces no results.

Down the hatch: This idiom can be said before drinking alcohol in company.

Down the pan: If something has gone down the pan, it has failed or been ruined.

Down the tubes: If something has gone down the tubes, it has failed or been ruined.

Down to the wire: (USA) If something goes down to the wire, like a competition, then it goes to the very last moment before it is clear who has won.

Down-to-earth: Someone who's down-to-earth is practical and realistic. It can also be used for things like ideas.

Drag your feet: If someone is dragging their feet, they are taking too long to do or finish something, usually because they don't want to do it.

Drag your heels: If you drag your heels, you either delay doing something or do it as slowly as possible because you don't want to do it.

Draw a blank: If you try to find something out and draw a blank, you don't get any useful information.

Draw a line in the sand: If you draw a line in the sand, you establish a limit beyond which things will be unacceptable.

Draw a long bow: If someone draws a long bow, they lie or exaggerate.

Draw the line: When you draw the line, you set out limits of what you find acceptable, beyond which you will not go.

Draw the shortest straw: If someone draws the shortest straw, they lose or are chosen to do something unpleasant.

Drive a wedge: If you drive a wedge between people, you exploit an issue so that people start to disagree.

Drive home: The idiomatic expression 'drive home' means 'reinforce' as in 'The company offered unlimited technical support as a way to drive home the message that customer satisfaction was its highest priority.'

Drive someone up the wall: If something or someone drives you up the wall, they do something that irritates you greatly.

Drive you spare: If someone or something drives you spare, it is extremely annoying.

Driven by a motor: This is used to describe people with Attention Deficit Hyperactivity Disorder when they talk excessively: 'they act as if driven by a motor.'

Drop a bombshell: If someone drops a bombshell, they announce something that changes a situation drastically and unexpectedly.

Drop a dime: (USA) If you tell someone to drop a dime, you're suggesting he or she telephone you at some future time.

Drop in the bucket: (USA) A drop in the bucket is something so small that it won't make any noticeable difference.

Drop like flies: This means that something is disappearing very quickly. For example, if you said people were dropping like flies, it would mean that they were dying off, quitting or giving up something rapidly.

Drop someone a line: If you drop someone a line, you send a letter to them.

Drop the ball: If someone drops the ball, they are not doing their job or taking their responsibilities seriously enough and let something go wrong.

Dropped like a hot cake: If something is dropped like a hot cake, it is rejected or disposed of very quickly.

Drown your sorrows: If someone gets drunk or drinks a lot to try to stop feeling unhappy, they drown their sorrows.

Drunk as a lord: (UK) Someone who is very drunk is as drunk as a lord.

Drunker than a peach orchard boar: (USA) Southern US expression - Very drunk, as when a boar would eat fermented peaches that have fallen from the tree.

Dry as a bone: If your lawn is as dry as a bone, the soil is completely dry.

Dry run: A dry run is a full rehearsal or trial exercise of something to see how it will work before it is launched.

Dry spell: If something or someone is having a dry spell, they aren't being as successful as they normally are.

Duck soup: (USA) If something is duck soup, it is very easy.

Duck to water: If you take to something like a duck to water, you find when you start that you have a natural affinity for it.

Ducks in a row: (USA) If you have your ducks in a row, you are well-organised.

Dull as ditchwater: (UK) If something is as dull as ditchwater, it is incredibly boring. A ditch is a long narrow hole or trench dug to contain water, which is normally a dark, dirty colour and stagnant.

Dumb as a rock: If you are dumb as a rock, you have no common sense and are stupid.

Dunkirk spirit: (UK) Dunkirk spirit is when people pull together to get through a very difficult time.

Dutch auction: If something is sold by setting a price, then reducing it until someone buys it, it is sold in a Dutch auction. It can also mean that something is changed until it is accepted by everyone.

Dutch courage: Dutch courage is the reckless bravery caused by drinking too much.

Dutch treat: If something like a meal is a Dutch treat, then each person pays their own share of the bill.

Dutch uncle: A Dutch uncle is a person who gives unwelcome advice.

Dutch wife: A Dutch wife is a long pillow or a hot water bottle.

Dwell on the past: Thinking too much about the past, so that it becomes a problem is to dwell on the past.

Dyed-in-the-wool: If someone is a dyed-in-the-wool supporter of a political party, etc, they support them totally, without any questions.

E

Each to their own: Different people have different preferences. In American English, 'Each to his own' is more common.

Eager beaver: A person who is extremely keen is an eager beaver.

Eagle eyes: Someone who has eagle eyes sees everything; no detail is too small.

Early bath: (UK) If someone has or goes for an early bath, they quit or lose their job or position earlier than expected because things have gone wrong.

Early bird catches the worm: The early bird catches the worm means that if you start something early, you stand a better chance of success.

Early to bed, early to rise, makes a man healthy wealthy and wise: It means that sleeping well and not staying up late will help you out physically and financially.

Earn a living: To make money Ex: We need to get a good job to earn a decent living.

Easier said than done: If something is easier said than done, it is much more difficult than it sounds. It is often used when someone advises you to do something difficult and tries to make it sound easy.

Easy as ABC: Something that is as easy as ABC is very easy or simple.

Easy as beans: Something that is so easy that anyone can do it is easy as beans.

Easy as pie: If something is easy as pie, it is very easy indeed.

Easy come, easy go: This idiom means that money or other material gains that come without much effort tend to get spent or consumed as easily.

Easy peasy: (UK) If something is easy peasy, it is very easy indeed.

Eat crow: (USA) If you eat crow, you have to admit that you were wrong about something.

Eat humble pie: If someone apologises and shows a lot of contrition for something they have done, they eat humble pie.

Eat like a bird: If someone eats like a bird, they eat very little.

Eat like a horse: Someone who eats like a horse, eats a lot.

Eat like a pig: If some eats like a pig, they either eat too much or they have bad table manners.

Eat my hat: People say this when they don't believe that something is going to happen e.g. 'If he passes that exam, I'll eat my hat!'

Eat someone alive: If you eat someone alive, you defeat or beat them comprehensively.

Eat your heart out: If someone tells you to eat your heart out, they are saying they are better than you at something.

Eat your words: If you eat your words, you accept publicly that you were wrong about something you said.

Economical with the truth: (UK) If someone, especially a politician, is economical with the truth, they leave out information in order to create a false picture of a situation, without actually lying.

Egg on your face: If someone has egg on their face, they are made to look foolish or embarrassed.

Elbow grease: If something requires elbow grease, it involves a lot of hard physical work.

Elbow room: If you haven't got enough elbow room, you haven't got enough space.

Elephant in the room: An elephant in the room is a problem that everyone knows very well but no one talks about because it is taboo, embarrassing, etc.

Eleventh hour: If something happens at the eleventh hour, it happens right at the last minute.

Empty vessels make the most noise: The thoughtless often speak the most.

End in smoke: If something ends in smoke, it produces no concrete or positive result. This expression refers to the boasting by a person, of having put in a lot of efforts by him, for a particular cause or to attain a result which is very difficult to be done by any person.

Even a blind squirrel finds a nut once in a while: This expression means that even if people are ineffective or misguided, sometimes they can still be correct just by being lucky.

Even a broken clock is right twice a day: This is used when people get lucky and are undeservedly successful.

Even keel: If something is on an even keel, it is balanced.

Even Stevens: If everything is equal between people, they are even Stevens.

Even the dogs in the street know: (Irish) This idiom is used frequently in Ireland, and means something is so obvious that even the dogs in the street know it.

Every ass likes to hear himself bray: This means that people like the sound of their own voice.

Every cloud has a silver lining: People sometimes say that every cloud has a silver lining to comfort somebody who's having problems. They mean that it is always possible to get something positive out of a situation, no matter how unpleasant, difficult or even painful it might seem.

Every dog has its day: This idiom means that everyone gets their moment to shine.

Every man and his dog: A lot of people - as in sending out invitations to a large number of people

Every man for himself: If it's every man for himself, then people are trying to save themselves from a difficult situation without trying to help anyone else.

Every man has his price: Anyone's opinion or support can be bought, everyone's principles have a limit.

Every man jack: If every man jack was involved in something, it is an emphatic way of saying that absolutely everybody was involved.

Every nook and cranny: If you search every nook and cranny, you look everywhere for something.

Every Tom, Dick and Harry: If every Tom, Dick and Harry knows about something, then it is common knowledge.

Every trick in the book: If you try every trick in the book, you try every possible way, including dishonesty and deceit, to get what you want.

Everybody and their uncle: This basically means a lot of people or too many people; everybody and their uncle was there.

Everything but the kitchen sink: If people include everything but the kitchen sink, they include every possibility, regardless of whether they are useful.

Exception that proves the rule: This expression is used by many to indicate that an exception in some way confirms a rule. Others say that the exception tests the rule. In its original legal sense, it meant that a rule could sometimes be inferred from an exemption or exception. In general use, the first meaning predominates nowadays, much to the annoyance of some pedants.

Explore all avenues: If all avenues are being explored, then every conceivable approach is being tried that could possibly get the desired result.

Eye candy: When a person is very attractive, they can be described as eye candy - sweet to look at!

Eye for an eye: This is an expression for retributive justice, where the punishment equals the crime.

Eye- wash: This expression 'eye-wash' is generally used to cover up the anxiety of a person who is seeking a concrete reply or justification for an act or an event that had affected his personal image or caused him a loss. The affected person usually represents his case to the higher-ups and puts forth his demands for redressal. But the authority, in order to avoid embarassment to his organisation or to himself, is not in a position to expose the entire material or evidence which in turn tell upon the credibility of the organisation. In such circumstances, he will usually call for an investigation to satisfy the complainant, but will not be keen in disposing the case. The authority will drag on the issue, (at the same time pretending to be serious) until the seriousness of the issue dies down and no finality is reached. So, ' The investigation on the issue by the authority is an eye-wash'.

F

Face like thunder: If someone has a face like thunder they are clearly very angry or upset about something.

Face only a mother could love: When someone has a face only a mother could love, they are ugly.

Face the music: If you have to face the music, you have to accept the negative consequences of something you have done wrong.

Face value: If you take something at face value, you accept the appearance rather than looking deeper into the matter.

Face your demons: If you face your demons, you confront your fears or something that you have been trying hard to avoid.

Facts of life: When someone is taught the facts of life, they learn about sex and reproduction.

Failure is the mother of success: Failure is often a stepping stone towards success.

Faint heart never won fair lady: This means that you will not get the partner of your dreams if you lack the confidence to let them know how you feel.

Fair and square: If someone wins something fair and square, they follow the rules and win conclusively.

Fair crack of the whip: (UK) If everybody has a fair crack of the whip, they all have equal opportunities to do something.

Fair shake of the whip: (USA) If everybody has a fair shake of the whip, they all have equal opportunities to do something.

Fair thee well: Meaning completely and fully: I am tied up today to a fair-thee-well.

Fairweather friend: A fairweather friend is the type who is always there when times are good but forgets about you when things get difficult or problems crop up.

Fall by the wayside: To fall by the wayside is to give up or fail before completion.

Fall from grace: If a person falls from grace, they lose favor with someone.

Fall off the wagon: If someone falls off the wagon, they start drinking after having given up completely for a time.

Fall on our feet: If you fall on your feet, you succeed in doing something where there was a risk of failure.

Fall on your sword: If someone falls on their sword, they resign or accept the consequences of some wrongdoing.

Familiarity breeds contempt: This means that the more you know something or someone, the more you start to find faults and dislike things about it or them.

Famous last words: This expression is used as a way of showing disbelief, rejection or self-deprecation.'They said we had no chance of winning- famous last words!'

Fast and furious: Things that happen fast and furious happen very quickly without stopping or pausing.

Fat cat: A fat cat is a person who makes a lot of money and enjoys a privileged position in society.

Fat chance!: This idiom is a way of telling someone they have no chance.

Fat head: A fat head is a dull, stupid person.

Fat hits the fire: When the fat hits the fire, trouble breaks out.

Fat of the land: Living off the fat of the land means having the best of everything in life.

Fate worse than death: Describing something as a fate worse than death is a fairly common way of implying that it is unpleasant.

Feast today, famine tomorrow: If you indulge yourself with all that you have today, you may have to go without tomorrow.

Feather in your cap: A success or achievement that may help you in the future is a feather in your cap.

Feather your own nest: If someone feathers their own nest, they use their position or job for personal gain.

Feathers fly: When people are fighting or arguing angrily, we can say that feathers are flying.

Fed up to the back teeth: When you are extremely irritated and fed up with something or someone, you are fed up to the back teeth.

Feel at home: If you feel relaxed and comfortable somewhere or with someone, you feel at home.

Feel free: If you ask for permission to do something and are told to feel free, the other person means that there is absolutely no problem

Feel like a million: If you feel like a million, you are feeling very well (healthy) and happy.

Feel the pinch: If someone is short of money or feeling restricted in some other way, they are feeling the pinch.

Feeling blue: If you feel blue, you are feeling unwell, mainly associated with depression or unhappiness.

Feet of clay: If someone has feet of clay, they have flaws that make them seem more human and like normal people.

Feet on the ground: A practical and realistic person has their feet on the ground.

Fence sitter: Someone that try to support both side of an argument without committing to either is a fence sitter.

Fiddle while Rome burns: If people are fiddling while Rome burns, they are wasting their time on futile things while problems threaten to destroy them.

Fine tuning: Small adjustments to improve something or to get it working are called fine tuning.

Fine words butter no parsnips: This idiom means that it's easy to talk, but talk is not action.

Finger in the pie: If you have a finger in the pie, you have an interest in something.

Fingers and thumbs: If you are all fingers and thumbs, you are being clumsy and not very skilled with your hands.

Fire away: If you want to ask someone a question and they tell you to fire away, they mean that you are free to ask what you want.

Fire on all cylinders: If something is firing on all cylinders, it is going as well as it could.

First come, first served: This means there will be no preferential treatment and a service will be provided to those that arrive first.

First out of the gate: When someone is first out of the gate, they are the first to do something that others are trying to do.

First port of call: The first place you stop to do something is your first port of call.

Fish in troubled waters: Someone who fishes in troubled waters tries to takes advantage of a shaky or unstable situation. The extremists were fishing in troubled waters during the political uncertainty in the country.

Fish or cut bait: (USA) This idiom is used when you want to tell someone that it is time to take action.

Fish out of water: If you are placed in a situation that is completely new to you and confuses you, you are like a fish out of water.

Fishy: If there is something fishy about someone or something, there is something suspicious; a feeling that there is something wrong, though it isn't clear what it is.

Fit as a fiddle: If you are fit as a fiddle, you are in perfect health.

Fit for a king: If something is fit for a king, it is of the very highest quality or standard.

Fit like a glove: If something fits like a glove, it is suitable or the right size.

Fit to be tied: If someone is fit to be tied, they are extremely angry.

Five o'clock shadow: A five o'clock shadow is the facial hair that a man gets if he doesn't shave for a day or two.

Flash in the pan: If something is a flash in the pan, it is very noticeable but doesn't last long, like most singers, who are very successful for a while, then forgotten.

Flat as a pancake: It is so flat that it is like a pancake- there is no head on that beer it is as flat as a pancake.

Flat out: If you work flat out, you work as hard and fast as you possibly can.

Fleet of foot: If someone is fleet of foot, they are very quick.

Flesh and blood: Your flesh and blood are your blood relatives, especially your immediate family.

Flogging a dead horse: (UK) If someone is trying to convince people to do or feel something without any hope of succeeding, they're flogging a dead horse. This is used when someone is trying to raise interest in an issue that no-one supports anymore; beating a dead horse will not make it do any more work.

Flowery speech: Flowery speech is full of lovely words, but may well lack substance.

Fly by the seat of one's pants: If you fly by the seat of one's pants, you do something difficult even though you don't have the experience or training required.

Fly in the ointment: A fly in the ointment is something that spoils or prevents complete enjoyment of something.

Fly off the handle: If someone flies off the handle, they get very angry.

Fly on the wall: If you are able to see and hear events as they happen, you are a fly on the wall.

Fly the coop: When children leave home to live away from their parents, they fly the coop.

Fly the coop: When someone flies the coop, they leave home and their family to start a new life.

Fly the flag: If someone flies the flag, they represent or support their country.

Food for thought: If something is food for thought, it is worth thinking about or considering seriously.

Fool me once, shame on you; fool me twice, shame on me: This means that you should learn from your mistakes and not allow people to take advantage of you repeatedly.

Fools rush in where angels fear to tread: This idiom is used where people who are inexperienced or lack knowledge do something that more informed people would avoid.

Foot in mouth: This is used to describe someone who has just said something embarrassing, inappropriate, wrong or stupid.

Foot in the door: If you have or get your foot in the door, you start working in a company or organisation at a low level, hoping that you will be able to progress from there.

Foot the bill: The person who foots the bill pays the bill for everybody.

Football's a game of two halves: (UK) If something's a game of two halves, it means that it's possible for someone's fortunes or luck to change and the person who's winning could end up a loser.

For a song: If you buy or sell something for a song, it is very cheap.

Fortune knocks once at every man's door: Everyone gets one good chance in a lifetime.

Foul play: If the police suspect foul play, they think a crime was committed.

Four corners of the earth: If something goes to, or comes from, the four corners of the earth, it goes or comes absolutely everywhere.

Four-eyes: A person who wears glasses

Four-square behind: If someone stands four-square behind someone, they give that person their full support.

Fourth estate: This is an idiomatic way of describing the media, especially the newspapers.

Free rein: If someone has a free rein, they have the authority to make the decisions they want without any restrictions.

Free-for-all: A free-for-all is a fight or contest in which everyone gets involved and rules are not respected.

Fresh from the oven: If something is fresh from the oven, it is very new.

Freudian Slip: If someone makes a Freudian slip, they accidentally use the wrong word, but in doing so reveal what they are really thinking rather than what they think the other person wants to hear.

Friendly footing: When relationships are on a friendly footing, they are going well.

From a different angle: If you look at something from a different angle, you look at it from a different point of view.

From pillar to post: If something is going from pillar to post, it is moving around in a meaningless way, from one disaster to another.

From rags to riches: Someone who starts life very poor and makes a fortune goes from rags to riches.

From scratch: This idiom means 'from the beginning'.

From soup to nuts: If you do something from soup to nuts, you do it from the beginning right to the very end.

From the bottom of your heart: If someone does something from the bottom of their heart, then they do it with genuine emotion and feeling.

From the horse's mouth: If you hear something from the horse's mouth, you hear it directly from the person concerned or responsible.

From the sublime to the ridiculous: If something declines considerably in quality or importance, it is said to have gone from the sublime to the ridiculous.

From the word go: From the word go means from the very beginning of something.

Full as a tick: If you are as full as a tick, you have eaten too much.

Full bore: If something is full bore, it involves the maximum effort or is complete and thorough.

Full circle: When something has come full circle, it has ended up where it started.

Full Monty: (UK) If something is the Full Monty, it is the real thing, not reduced in any way.

Full of beans: If someone's full of beans, they are very energetic.

Full of hot air: Someone who is full of hot air talks a lot of rubbish.

Full of oneself: Someone who acts in a arrogant or egotistical manner is full of himself/herself.

Full of piss and vinegar: Someone who's full of piss and vinegar is full of youthful energy.

Full of the joys of spring: If you are full of the joys of spring, you are very happy and full of energy.

Full swing: If a something is in full swing, it is going or doing well.

Fuzzy thinking: Thinking or ideas that do not agree with the facts or information available

G

Game on: When someone says 'Game on!', it means that they are accepting a challenge or ready to get something done.

Game plan: A game plan is a strategy.

Garbage fee: A garbage fee is a charge that has no value and doesn't provide any real service.

Garbage in, garbage out: If a computer system or database is built badly, then the results will be bad.

Gardening leave: (UK) If someone is paid for a period when they are not working, either after they have given in their notice or when they are being investigated, they are on gardening leave.

Gather pace: If events gather pace, they move faster.

Gather steam: If something gathers speed, it moves or progresses at an increasing speed.

Get a handle on: When you get a handle on something, you come to understand it.

Get along famously: If people get along famously, they have an exceedingly good relationship.

Get away scot-free: If someone gets away scot-free, they are not punished when they have done something wrong.

Get away with murder: If you get away with murder, you do something bad and don't get caught or punished.

Get back on the horse that bucked you: When you start drinking again after being hungover from drinking the previous night.

Get in on the act: If people want to get in on the act, they want to participate in something that is currently profitable or popular.

Get in on the ground floor: If you get in on the ground floor, you enter a project or venture at the start before people know how successful it might be.

Get it in the neck: (UK) If you get it in the neck, you are punished or criticised for something.

Get it off your chest: If you get something off your chest, you confess to something that has been troubling you.

Get on your soapbox: If someone on their soapbox, they hold forth (talk a lot) about a subject they feel strongly about.

Get out of bed on the wrong side: If you get out of bed on the wrong side, you wake up and start the day in a bad mood for no real reason.

Get the axe: If you get the axe, you lose your job.

Get the ball rolling: If you get the ball rolling, you start something so that it can start making progress.

Get the green light: If you get the green light to do something, you are given the necessary permission, authorisation.

Get the monkey off your back: If you get the monkey off your back, you pass on a problem to someone else.

Get the picture: If you get the picture, you understand a situation fully.

Get the show on the road: If you get the show on the road, you put a plan into operation or begin something.

Get to grips: If you get to grips with something, you take control and do it properly.

Get up and go: If someone has lots of get up and go, they have lots of enthusiasm and energy.

Get wind of: If you get wind of something, you hear or learn about it, especially if it was meant to be secret.

Get your ducks in a row: If you get your ducks in a row, you organise yourself and your life.

Get your feathers in a bunch: If you get your feathers in a bunch, you get upset or angry about something.

Get your feet wet: If you get your feet wet, you gain your first experience of something.

Get your goat: If something gets your goat, it annoys you.

Get your hands dirty: If you get your hands dirty, you become involved in something where the realities might compromise your principles. It can also mean that a person is not just stuck in an ivory tower dictating strategy, but is prepared to put in the effort and hard work to make the details actually happen.

Get your head around something: If you get your head around something, you come to understand it even though it is difficult to comprehend.

Get your teeth into: If you get your teeth into something, you become involved in or do something that is intellectually challenging or satisfying.

Get your wires crossed: If people get their wires cross, they misunderstand each other, especially when making arrangements.

Ghost of a chance: If something or someone hasn't got a ghost of a chance, they have no hope whatsoever of succeeding.

Ghostly presence: You can feel or otherwise sense a ghostly presence, but you cannot do it clearly only vaguely.

Gift of the gab: If someone has the gift of the gab, they speak in a persuasive and interesting way.

Gild the lily: If you gild the lily, you decorate something that is already ornate.

Gilded cage: If someone is in a gilded cage, they are trapped and have restricted or no freedom, but have very comfortable surroundings- many famous people live in luxury but cannot walk out of their house alone.

Girl Friday: A girl Friday is a female employee who assists someone without any specific duties.

Give a big hand: Applaud by clapping hands. 'Let's give all the contestents a big hand.'

Give a dog a bad name: A person who is generally known to have been guilty of some offence will always be suspected to be the author of all similar types of offence. Once someone has gained a bad reputation, it is very difficult to lose it.

Give and take: Where there is give and take, people make concessions in order to get things they want in negotiations.

Give as good as you get: If you give as good as you get, you are prepared to treat people as badly as they treat you and to fight for what you believe.

Give it some stick: (UK) If you give something some stick, you put a lot of effort into it.

Give me a hand: If someone gives you a hand, they help you.

Give me five: If someone says this, they want to hit your open hand against theirs as a way of congratulation or greeting.

Give someone a leg up: If you give someone a leg up, you help them to achieve something that they couldn't have done alone.

Give someone a piece of your mind: If you give someone a piece of your mind, you criticise them strongly and angrily.

Give someone a run for their money: If you can give someone a run for the money, you are as good,

Give someone enough rope: If you give someone enough rope, you give them the chance to get themselves into trouble or expose themselves.

Give someone stick: (UK) If someone gives you stick, they criticise you or punish you.

Give someone the runaround: If someone gives you the runaround, they make excuses and give you false explanations to avoid doing something.

Give the nod: (UK) If you give the nod to something, you approve it or give permission to do it.

Give up the ghost: People give up the ghost when they die. Machines stop working when they give up the ghost.

Give your eye teeth: If you really want something and would be prepared to sacrifice a lot to get it, you would give your eye teeth for it.

Given the day that's in it: (Irish) This idiom is used when something is obvious because of the day that it occurs: traffic, for example would be busy around a football stadium on game day, given the day that's in it. On any other day the traffic would be unexplainable, but because its game day its obvious why there is traffic.

Glass ceiling: The glass ceiling is the discrimination that prevents women and minorities from getting promoted to the highest levels of companies and organisations.

Gloves are off: When the gloves are off, people start to argue or fight in a more serious way.

Glutton for punishment: If a person is described as a glutton for punishment, the happily accept jobs and tasks that most people would try to get out of. A glutton is a person who eats a lot.

Gnaw your vitals: If something gnaws your vitals, it troubles you greatly and affects you at a very deep level.

Go against the grain: A person who does things in an unconventional manner, especially if their methods are not generally approved of, is said to go against the grain. Such an individual can be called a maverick.

Go awry: If things go awry, they go wrong.

Go bananas: If you go bananas, you are wild with excitement, anxiety, or worry.

Go blue: If you go blue, you are very cold indeed.

Go bust: If a company goes bust, it goes bankrupt.

Go by the board: When something has gone by the board, it no longer exists or an opportunity has been lost.

Go by the boards: If something goes by the boards, it fails to get approved or accepted.

Go down like a lead balloon: (UK) If something goes down like a lead balloon, it fails or is extremely badly received.

Go down swinging: If you want to go down swinging, you know you will probably fail, but you refuse to give up.

Go down without a fight: If someone goes down without a fight, they surrender without putting up any resistance.

Go Dutch: If you go Dutch in a restaurant, you pay equal shares for the meal.

Go fly a kite: (USA) This is used to tell someone to go away and leave you alone.

Go for broke: If someone goes for broke, they risk everything they have for a potentially greater gain.

Go fry an egg: (USA) This is used to tell someone to go away and leave you alone.

Go hand in hand: If things go hand in hand, they are associated and go together.

Go nuts: If someone goes nuts, they get excited over something.

Go off on a tangent: If someone goes off on a tangent, they change the subject completely in the middle of a conversation or talk.

Go over like a lead balloon: (USA) If something goes over like a lead balloon, it will not work well, or go over well.

Go overboard: If you go overboard, you do something excessively.

Go pear-shaped: If things have gone wrong, they have gone pear-shaped.

Go play in traffic: This is used as a way of telling someone to go away.

Go round in circles: If people are going round in circles, they keep discussing the same thing without reaching any agreement or coming to a conclusion.

Go south: If things go south, they get worse or go wrong.

Go spare: (UK) If you go spare, you lose your temper completely.

Go tell it to birds: This is used when someone says something that is not credible or is a lie.

Go the distance: If you go the distance, you continue until something ends, no matter how difficult.

Go the extra mile: If someone is prepared to go the extra mile, they will do everything they can to help or to make something succeed, going beyond their duty what could be expected of them .

Go the whole hog: If you go the whole hog, you do something completely or to its limits.

Go through the motions: When you go through the motions, you do something like an everyday routine and without any feelings whatsoever.

Go to seed: If someone has gone to seed, they have declined in quality or appearance.

Go to the wire: If someone goes to the wire, they risk their life, job, reputation, etc, to help someone.

Go to your head: If something goes to your head, it makes you feel vain. If alcohol goes to your head, it makes you feel drunk quickly.

Go under the hammer: If something goes under the hammer, it is sold in an auction.

Go west: If something goes west, it goes wrong. If someone goes west, they die.

Going concern: A successful and active business is a going concern.

Going overboard: If you go overboard with something, then you take something too far, or do too much.

Golden handshake: A golden handshake is a payment made to someone to get them to leave their job.

Golden rule: The golden rule is the most essential or fundamental rule associated with something. Originally, it was not a general reference to an all purpose first rule applicable to many groups or protocols, but referred to a verse in the Bible about treating people they way you would want them to treat you, which was considered the First Rule of behavior towards all by all.

Golden touch: Someone with a golden touch can make money from or be successful at anything they do.

Gone fishing: If someone has gone fishing, they are not very aware of what is happening around them.

Gone for a burton: (UK) If something's gone for a burton, it has been spoiled or ruined. If a person has gone for a burton, they are either in serious trouble or have died.

Gone pear-shaped: (UK) If things have gone pear-shaped they have either gone wrong or produced an unexpected and unwanted result.

Gone to pot: If something has gone to pot, it has gone wrong and doesn't work any more.

Gone to the dogs: If something has gone to the dogs, it has gone badly wrong and lost all the good things it had.

Good antennae: Someone with good antennae is good at detecting things.

Good as gold: If children are as good as gold, they behave very well.

Good egg: A person who can be relied on is a good egg. Bad egg is the opposite.

Good fences make good neighbours: This means that it is better for people to mind their own business and to respect the privacy of others.

Good hand: If you are a good hand at something, you do it well.

Good Samaritan: A good Samaritan is a persoon wh helps others in need.

Good shape: If something's in good shape, it's in good condition. If a person's in good shape, they are fit and healthy.

Good spell: A spell can mean a fairly or relatively short period of time; you'll hear weather forecasts predict a dry spell. Sports commentators will say that a sportsperson is going through a good spell when they're performing consistently better than they normally do.

Good time: If you make good time on a journey, you manage to travel faster than you expected.

Good to go: Someone or something that meets one's approval. 'He is good to go.' 'The idea you had is good to go.'

Good walls make good neighbours: Your relationship with your neighbours depends, among other things, on respecting one another's privacy.

Goody two-shoes: A goody two-shoes is a self-righteous person who makes a great deal of their virtue.

Grab the bulls by its horns: If you grab (take) the bull by its horns, you deal head-on and directly with a problem.

Grain of salt: If you should take something with a grain of salt, you shouldn't necessarily believe it all.

Grasp the nettle: (UK) If you grasp the nettle, you deal bravely with a problem.

Grass may be greener on the other side but it's just as hard to mow: 'The grass may be greener on the other side but it's just as hard to mow' is an expression used to mean a person's desire to have that which another person has in the belief it will make their life easieris false as all situations come with their own set of problems.

Grass roots: This idioms is often used in politics, where it refers to the ordinary people or voters. It can be used to mean people at the bottom of a hierarchy.

Grass widow: A grass widow is a woman whose husband is often away on work, leaving her on her own.

Graveyard shift: If you have to work very late at night, it is the graveyard shift.

Gravy train: If someone is on the gravy train, they have found and easy way to make lots of money.

Grease monkey: A grease monkey is an idiomatic term for a mechanic.

Grease someone's palm: If you grease someone's palm, you bribe them to do something.

Grease the skids: If you grease the skids, you facilitate something.

Greased lightning: If something or someone moves like greased lightning, they move very fast indeed.

Great guns: If something or someone is going great guns, they are doing very well.

Great Scott: An exclamation of surprise.

Great unwashed: This is a term used for the working class masses.

Great white hope: Someone who is expected to be a great success is a great white hope.

Greek to me: If you don't understand something, it's all Greek to you.

Green around the gills: If someone looks green around the gills, they look ill.

Green fingers: (UK) Someone with green fingers has a talent for gardening.

Green light: If you are given the green light, you are given approval to do something.

Green thumb: (USA) Someone with a talent for gardening has a green thumb.

Grey area: A grey/gray area is one where there is no clear right or wrong.

Grey Cardinal: Someone who is a Grey Cardinal exerts power behind the scenes, without drawing attention to himself or herself.

Grey cells: 'Grey cells' means 'brain' Eg: Use your grey cells to understand it

Grey matter: Grey/gray matter is the human brain.

Grey pound: (UK) In the UK, the grey pound is an idiom for the economic power of elderly people.

Grey suits: The men in grey suits are people who have a lot of power in business or politics, but aren't well-known or charismatic.

Grin and bear it: If you have to grin and bear it, you have to accept something that you don't like.

Grin like a Cheshire cat: If someone has a very wide smile, they have a grin like a Cheshire cat.

Grinds my gear: Something that is very annoying grinds your gear.

Grist for the mill: Something that you can use to your advantage is grist for the mill.

Guinea-pig: If you are a guinea-pig, you take part in an experiment of some sort and are used in the testing.

Gunboat diplomacy: If a nation conducts its diplomatic relations by threatening military action to get what it wants, it is using gunboat diplomacy.

Gung ho: If someone is gung ho about something, they support it blindly and don't think about the consequences.

H

Hail-fellow-well-met: Someone whose behavior is hearty, friendly and congenial.

Hair of the dog: If someone has a hair of the dog, they have an alcoholic drink as a way of getting rid of a hangover, the unpleasant effects of having drunk too much alcohol the night before. It is commonly used as a way of excusing having a drink early on in the day.

Hairy at the heel: (UK) Someone who is hairy at the heel is dangerous or untrustworthy.

Hale and hearty: Someone who is hale and hearty is in very good health.

Half a mind: If you have half a mind to do something, you haven't decided to do it, but are thinking seriously about doing it.

Half-baked: A half-baked idea or scheme hasn't not been thought through or planned very well.

Hammer and tongs: If people are going at it hammer and tongs, they are arguing fiercely. The idiom can also be used hen people are doing something energetically.

Hand in glove: If people are hand in glove, they have an extremely close relationship.

Hand in hand: Hand in hand= work together closely When people in a group, say in an office or in a project, work together with mutual understanding to achieve the target, we say they work hand in hand. There is no lack of co-operation and each synchoranises the activity with that of the other.

Hand that rocks the cradle: Women have a great power and influence because they have the greatest influence over the development of children- the hand that rocks the cradle.

Hand to mouth: Someone who's living from hand to mouth, is very poor and needs the little money they have coming in to cover their expenses.

Hands down: If someone is better hands down than everyone else, they are much better.

Handwriting like chicken scratch: If your handwriting is very hard to read, it is like chicken scratch.

Hang by a thread: If something hangs by a thread, there is a very small chance indeed of it being successful or surviving.

Hang in the balance: If an outcome is hanging in the balance, there are at least two possibilities and it is impossible to predict which will win out.

Hang out to dry: If you hang someone out to dry, you abandon them when they are in trouble.

Hangdog expression: A hangdog expression is one where the person's showing their emotions very clearly, maybe a little too clearly for your liking. It's that mixture of misery and self-pity that is similar to a dog when it's trying to get something it wants but daren't take without permission.

Hanged for a sheep as a lamb: This is an expression meaning that if you are going to get into trouble for doing something, then you ought to stop worrying and should try to get everything you can before you get caught.

Happy medium: If you reach a happy medium, you are making a compromise; reaching a conclusion or decision.

Hard as nails: A person who is as hard as nails is either physically tough or has little or no respect for other people's feelings.

Hard by: "Hard by" means mean "close to" or "near".

Hard cheese: (UK) Hard cheese means hard luck.

Hard of hearing: Someone who's hard of hearing is a bit deaf.

Hard on someone's heels: If you are hard on someone's heels, you are close to them and trying to catch or overtake them.

Hard sell: If someone puts a lot of pressure on you to do or buy something, they are hard selling it.

Hard to come by: If something is hard to come by, it is difficult to find.

Hard up: If you are hard up, you have very little money.

Haste makes waste: This idiom means that if you try to do something quickly, without planning it, you're likely to end up spending more time, money, etc, doing it.

Hat trick: Three successes one after the other is a hat trick.

Hatchet job: A piece of criticism that destroys someone's reputation is a hatchet job.

Have a ball: If you have a ball, you have a great time, a lot of fun.

Have a bash: If you have a bash at something, you try to do it, especially when there isn't much chance of success.

Have a blast: It means "to have a lot of fun".

Have a go: If you have a go, you try to do something, often when you don't think you have much chance of succeeding.

Have a heart: If someone has a heart, they arekind and sympathetic. If you say, 'Have a heart' to someone, you are asking them to be understanding and sympathetic.

Have a ripper: If you have a ripper of a time, you enjoy yourself.

Have a trick up your sleeve: If you have a trick up your sleeve, you have a secret strategy to use when the time is right.

Have no truck with: If you have no truck with something or someone, you refuse to get involved with it or them.

Have the floor: If someone has the floor, it is their turn to speak at a meeting.

Have the guts: Someone who has enough courage to do something has the guts to do it.

Have your cake and eat it too: If someone wants to have their cake and eat it too, they want everything their way, especially when their wishes are contradictory.

Have your collar felt: If someone has their collar felt, they are arrested.

Have your fill: If you have had your fill, you are fed up of somebody or something.

Have your lunch handed to you: If you have you lunch handed to you, you are outperformed and shown up by someone better.

Have your moments: Someone who has his or her moments exhibits a positive behavior pattern on an occasional basis but not generally.

Have your tail up: If someone has their tail up, they are optimistic and expect to be successful.

Have your work cut out: If you have your work cut out, you are very busy indeed.

Having a gas: If you're having a gas, you are having a laugh and enjoying yourself in company.

Hay is for horses: This idiom is used as a way of telling children not to say the word 'hey' as in hey you or hey there.

He that travels far knows much: People who travel widely have a wide knowledge.

He who hesitates is lost: If one waits too long, the opportunity vanishes.

Head for the hills: If people head for the hills, they run away from trouble.

Head is in the clouds: If a person has their head in the clouds, they have unrealistic, impractical ideas.

Head is mince: (Scot) When someone's thoughts are in a state of abject confusion, especially when facing a severe dilemma, their head is mince.

Head nor tail: If you can't make head nor tail of something, you cannot understand it at all or make any sense of it.

Head on a spike: If someone wants a head on a spike, they want to be able to destroy or really punish a person.

Head on the block: If someone's head is on the block, they are going to be held responsible and suffer the consequences for something that has gone wrong.

Head over heels in love: When someone falls passionately in love and is intoxicated by the feeling has fallen head over heels in love.

Head south: If something head south, it begins to fail or start going bad.'The project proceeded well for the first two months, but then it headed south.'

Heads will roll: If heads will roll, people will be punished or sacked for something that has gone wrong.

Heads-up: A heads-up is advanced information or a warning

Headstrong: A headstrong person is obstinate and does not take other people's advice readily.

Healthy as a horse: If you're as healthy as a horse, you're very healthy.

Heap coals on someone's head: To do something nice or kind to someone who has been nasty to you. If someone felt bad because they forgot to get you a Christmas gift, for you to buy them a specially nice gift is heaping coals on their head.

Hear a pin drop: If there is complete silence in a room, you can hear a pin drop.

Hear on the grapevine: To receive information indirectly through a series of third parties, similar to a rumour.

Heart in the right place: If someone's heart is in the right place, they are good and kind, though they might not always appear to be so.

Heart in the right place: If someone's heart is in the right place, their intentions are good even if they mess things up.

Heart in your boots: If you're heart is in your boots, you are very unhappy.

Heart in your mouth: If your heart is in your mouth, then you feel nervous or scared.

Heart isn't in it: If your heart is not in something, then you don't really believe in it or support it.

Heart misses a beat: If your heart misses a beat, you are suddenly shocked or surprised.

Heart of glass: When someone has a heart of glass, they are easily affected emotionally.

Heart of gold: Someone with a heart of gold is a genuinely kind and caring person.

Heart of steel: When someone has a heart of steel, they do not show emotion or are not affected emotionally.

Heart-to-heart: A heart-to-heart is a frank and honest conversation with someone, where you talk honestly and plainly about issues, no matter how painful.

Heaven knows: If you ask someone a question and they say this, they have no idea.

Heavenly bodies: The heavenly bodies are the stars.

Heavy-handed: If someone is heavy-handed, they are insensitive and use excessive force or authority when dealing with a problem.

Hedge your bets: If you hedge your bets, you don't risk everything on one opportunity, but try more than one thing.

Hell for leather: If you do something hell for leather, especially running, you do it as fast as you can.

Hell in a handcart: If something is going to hell in a handcart, it is getting worse and worse, with no hope of stopping the decline.

Herding cats: If you have to try to co-ordinate a very difficult situation, where people want to do very different things, you are herding cats.

Here today, gone tomorrow: Money, happiness and other desirable things are often here today, gone tomorrow, which means that they don't last for very long.

Hide nor hair: When there's no trace of something or a person, you haven't seen hide nor hair of it or them.

Hiding to nothing: If people are on a hiding to nothing, their schemes and plans have no chance of succeeding. 'Hiding to nowhere' is an alternative.

High and dry: If you are left high and dry, you are left alone and given no help at all when you need it.

High and low: If you search high and low, you look everywhere for something or someone.

High and mighty: The high and mighty are the people with authority and power. If a person is high and mighty, they behave in a superior and condescending way.

High as a kite: If someone's as high as a kite, it means they have had too much to drink or are under the influence of drugs.

Hit the road: When people hit the road, they leave a place to go somewhere else.

Hit the roof: If you lose your temper and get very angry, you hit the roof.

Hit the sack: When you hit the sack, you go to bed.

Hive of worker bees: A hive of worker bees is a group of people working actively and cooperatively. Example: The classroom was a hive of worker bees.

Hobson's choice: A Hobson's choice is something that appears to be a free choice, but is really no choice as there is no genuine alternative.

Hoist with your own petard: If you are hoist with your own petard, you get into trouble or caught in a trap that you had set for someone else.

Hold all the aces: If you hold all the aces, you have all the advantages and your opponents or rivals are in a weak position.

Hold the baby: (UK) If someone is responsible for something, they are holding the baby.

Hold the bag: (USA) If someone is responsible for something, they are holding the bag.

Hold the fort: If you hold the fort, you look after something or assume someone's responsibilities while they are away.

Hold the torch: If you hold the torch for someone, you have an unrequited or unspoken love.

Hold water: When you say that something does or does not 'hold water', it means that the point of view or argument put forward is or is not sound, strong or logical. For e.g., 'Saying we should increase our interest rates because everyone else is doing so will not hold water'.

Hold your horses: If someone tells you to hold your horses, you are doing something too fast and they would like you to slow down.

Hold your own: If you can hold your own, you can compete or perform equally with other people.

Hold your tongue: If you hold your tongue, you keep silent even though you want to speak.

Holier-than-thou: Someone who is holier-than-thou believes that they are morally superior to other people.

Hollow leg: Someone who has a hollow leg eats what seems to be more than his stomach can hold.

Hollow victory: A hollow victory is where someone wins something in name, but are seen not to have gained anything by winning.

Holy smoke!: This is a way of expressing surprise: "Holy smoke! Look at all of those geese!"

Home and hearth: 'Home and hearth' is an idiom evoking warmth and security.

Home is where you lay your hat: Wherever you are comfortable and at ease with yourself is your home, regardless where you were born or brought up.

Home stretch: The home stretch is the last part of something, like a journey, race or project.

Home sweet home: This is said when one is pleased to be back at one's own home.

Home, James: (UK) This is a cliched way of telling the driver of a vehicle to start driving. It is supposed to be an order to a chauffeur (a privately employed driver). The full phrase is 'Home, James, and don't spare the horses'.

Honest truth: If someone claims that something is the honest truth, they wish to sound extra-sincere about something.

Honor among thieves: If someone says there is honor among thieves, this means that even corrupt or bad people sometimes have a sense of honor or integrity, or justice, even if it is skewed.

Honours are even: If honours are even, then a competition has ended with neither side emerging as a winner.

Hook, line, and sinker: If somebody accepts or believes something hook, line, and sinker, they accept it completely.

Hop, skip, and a jump: If a place is a hop, skip, and a jump from somewhere, it's only a short distance away.

Hope against hope: If you hope against hope, you hope for something even though there is little or no chance of your wish being fulfilled.

Hope in hell: If something hasn't got a hope in hell, it stands absolutely no chance of succeeding.

Hornets' nest: A hornets' nest is a violent situation or one with a lot of dispute.

Horns of a dilemma: If you are on the horns of a dilemma, you are faced with two equally unpleasant options and have to choose one.

Horse of a different color: (USA) If something is a horse of a different color, it's a different matter or separate issue altogether.

Horse trading: Horse trading is an idiom used to describe negotiations, especially where these are difficult and involve a lot of compromise.

Horses for courses: Horses for courses means that what is suitable for one person or situation might be unsuitable for another.

Hostile takeover: If a company is bought out when it does not want to be, it is known as a hostile takeover.

Hot air: Language that is full of words but means little or nothing is hot air.

Hot as blue blazes: If something's as hot as blue blazes, it's extremely hot.

Hot water: If you get into hot water, you get into trouble.

Hot-blooded: Someone who is hot-blooded is easily excitable or passionate.

Hot-headed: A hot-headed person gets angry very easily.

Hour of need: A time when someone really needs something, almost a last chance, is their hour of need.

House of cards: Something that is poorly thought out and can easily collapse or fail is a house of cards.

How come

If you want to show disbelief or surprise about an action, you can ask a question using 'how come'. How come he got the job?

How do you like them apples: (USA) This idiomatic expression is used to express surprise or shock at something that has happened. It can also be used to boast about something you have done.

How long is a piece of string: If someone has no idea of the answer to a question, they can ask 'How long is a piece of string?' as a way of indicating their ignorance.

How's tricks?: This is used as a way of asking people how they are and how things have been going in their life.

Hungry as a bear: If you are hungry as a bear, it means that you are really hungry.

Hunky Dory: If something is hunky dory, it is perfectly satisfactory, fine.

I

I hereby give notice of my intention: Hereby is used sometimes in formal, official declarations and statements to give greater force to the speaker' or the writer's affirmation. People will say it sometimes to emphasise their sincerity and correctness.

I may be daft, but I'm not stupid: I might do or say silly things occasionally, but in this instance I know what I am doing.

I should cocoa: (UK) This idiom comes from 'I should think so', but is normally used sarcastically to mean the opposite.

I'll cross that road when I come to it: I'll think about something just when it happens, not in advance.

I'll eat my hat: You can say this when you are absolutely sure that you are right to let the other person know that there is no chance of your being wrong.

I've got a bone to pick with you: If somebody says this, they mean that they have some complaint to make against the person they are addressing.

I've got your number: You have made a mistake and I am going to call you on it. You are in trouble (a threat). I have a disagreement with you. I understand your true nature.

Icing on the cake: This expression is used to refer to something good that happens on top of an already good thing or situation.

If the cap fits, wear it: This idiom means that if the description is correct, then it is describing the truth, often when someone is being criticised.

If wishes were horses, beggars would ride: This means that wishing for something or wanting it is not the same as getting or having it.

If wishes were horses, beggars would ride: If we could have things the way we wanted them, then life would be much easier than it is.

If you can't stand the heat, get out of the kitchen: Originally a Harry S. Truman quote, this means that if you can't take the pressure, then you should remove yourself from the situation.

If you fly with the crows, you get shot with the crows: If you wish to be associated with a particular high risk and/or high profile situation and benefit from the rewards of that association, you have to accept the consequences if things go wrong - you cannot dissociate yourself.

If you lie down with dogs, you will get up with fleas: This means that if you become involved with bad company, there will be negative consequences.

If you lie down with the Devil, you will wake up in hell.: This means that if you become involved with bad company, there will be negative consequences.

If you will: 'If you will' is used as a way of making a concession in a sentence: He wasn't a very honest person, a liar if you will. Here, it is used a way of accepting that the reader or listener might think of the person as a liar, but without commit the writer or speaker to that position fully.

If you'll pardon my French: (UK) This idiom is used as a way of apologising for swearing.

Ill at ease: If someone is ill at ease, they are worried or uncomfortable.

Ill-gotten gains: Ill-gotten gains are profits or benefits that are made either illegally or unfairly.

In a cleft stick: If you are in a cleft stick, you are in a difficult situation, caught between choices.

In a fix: If you are in a fix, you are in trouble.

In a flash: If something happens in a flash, it happens very quickly indeed.

In a fog: If you're in a fog, you are confused, dazed or unaware.

In a heartbeat: If something happens very quickly or immediately, it happens in a heartbeat.

In a jam: If you are in a jam, you are in some trouble. If you get out of a jam, you avoid trouble.

In a jiffy: If something happens in a jiffy, it happens very quickly.

In a nutshell: This idiom is used to introduce a concise summary.

In a pickle: If you are in a pickle, you are in some trouble or a mess.

In a pickle: If you are in a pickle you are in some trouble or a mess.

In a rut: In a settled or established pattern, habit or course of action, especially a boring one.

In a tick: (UK) If someone will do something in a tick, they'll do it very soon or very quickly.

In a tight spot: If you're in a tight spot, you're in a difficult situation.

In all honesty: If you say something in all honesty, you are telling the complete truth. It can be used as a way of introducing a negative opinion whilst trying to be polite; in all honesty, I have to say that I wasn't very impressed.

In an instant: If something happens in an instant, it happens very rapidly.

In another's shoes: It is difficult to know what another person's life is really like, so we don't know what it is like to be in someone's shoes.

In apple-pie order: If something is in apple-pie order, it is very neat and organised.

In broad daylight: If a crime or problem happens in broad daylight, it happens during the day and should have been seen and stopped.

In cahoots: If people are in cahoots, they are conspiring together.

In cold blood: If something is done in cold blood, it is done ruthlessly, without any emotion.

In dire straits: If you're in dire straits, you're in serious trouble or difficulties.

In donkey's years: 'I haven't seen her in donkey's years.' - This means for a very long time.

In dribs and drabs: If people arrive in dribs and drabs, they come in small groups at irregular intervals, instead of all arriving at the same time.

In droves: When things happen in droves, a lot happen at the same time or very quickly.

In for a penny, in for a pound: If something is worth doing then it is a case of in for a penny, in for a pound, which means that when gambling or taking a chance, you might as well go the whole way and take all the risks, not just some.

In full swing: If things are in full swing, they have been going for a sufficient period of time to be going well and very actively.

In high gear: (USA) If something is in high gear, it is in a quick-paced mode. If someone is in high gear, they are feverishly on the fast track.

In high spirits: If someone is in high spirits, they are in a very good mood or feeling confident about something.

In hot water: If you are in hot water, you are in serious trouble.

In light of: 'In light of' is similar to 'due to'.

In like Flynn: Refers to Errol Flynn's popularity with women in the 40's. His ability to attract women was well known throughout the world.

In my bad books: If you are in someone's bad books, they are angry with you. Likewise, if you are in their good books, they are pleased with you.

In my book: This idiom means 'in my opinion'.

In my good books: If someone is in your good books, you are pleased with or think highly of them at the moment.

In one ear and out the other: If something goes in one ear and out the other, you forget it as soon as you've heard it because it was too complicated, boring etc.

In over your head: If someone is in over their head, they are out of the depth in something they are involved in, and may end up in a mess.

In perfect form: When something is as it ought to be. Or, when used cynically, it may refer to someone whose excesses are on display; a caricature.

In rude health: (UK) If someone's in rude health, they are very healthy and look it.

In so many words: This phrase may be used to mean 'approximately' or 'more or less'. I think it may have a sarcastic connotation in that the individual listening needed 'so many words' to get the point. It also may suggest the effort on the part of the speaker to explain an unpleasant truth or difficult concept.

In someone's pocket: If a person is in someone's pocket, they are dependent, especially financially, on them.

In spades: (UK) If you have something in spades, you have a lot of it.

In stitches: If someone is in stitches, they are laughing uncontrollably.

In tandem: If people do things in tandem, they do them at the same time.

In the bag: If something is in the bag, it is certain that you will get it or achieve it

In the ballpark: This means that something is close to the adequate or required value.

In the black: If your bank account is in credit, it is in the black.

In the cards: If something is in the cards, it is bound to occur, it is going to happen, or it is inevitable.

In the catbird seat: (USA) If someone is in the catbird seat, they are in an advantageous or superior position.

In the clear: If someone is in the clear, they are no longer suspected of or charged with wrongdoing.

In the clink: (UK) If someone is in the clink, they are in prison.

In the club: (UK) If a woman's in the club, she's pregnant. 'In the pudding club' is an alternative form.

In the dock: If someone is in the dock, they are on trial in court.

In the doghouse: If someone is in the doghouse, they are in disgrace and very unpopular at the moment.

In the driver's seat: If you are in the driver's seat, you are in charge of something or in control of a situation.

In the face of: If people act in the face of something, they do it despite it or when threatened by it.

In the family way: If a woman is in the family way, she is pregnant.

In the flesh: If you meet or see someone in the flesh you actually meet or see them, rather than seeing them on TV or in other media.

In the gravy: If you're in the gravy, you're rich and make money easily.

In the hole: If someone is in the hole, they have a lot of problems, especially financial ones.

In the hot seat: If someone's in the hot seat, they are the target for a lot of unwelcome criticism and examination.

In the know: If you are in the know, you have access to all the information about something, which other people don't have.

In the lap of luxury: People in the lap of luxury are very wealthy and have have everything that money can buy.

In the long run: This means 'over a long period of time', 'in the end' or 'in the final result'.

In the loop: If you're in the loop, you are fully informed about what is happening in a certain area or activity.

In the lurch: If you are left in the lurch, you are suddenly left in an embarrassing or tricky situation.

In the making: When something is in the making, it means it is in the process of being made.

In the offing: If something is in the offing, it is very likely to happen soon.

In the pink: If you are in very good health, you are in the pink.

In the pipeline: If something's in the pipeline, it hasn't arrived yet but its arrival is expected.

In the red: If your bank account is overdrawn, it is in the red.

In the saddle: If you're in the saddle, you are in control of a situation.

In the same boat: If people are in the same boat, they are in the same predicament or trouble.

In the short run: This refers to the immediate future.

In the soup: If you're in the soup, you're in trouble.

In the swim: If you are in the swim, you are up-to-date with and fully informed about something.

In the swing: If things are in the swing, they are progressing well.

In the tall cotton: A phrase that expresses good times or times of plenty and wealth as tall cotton means a good crop.

In the twinkling of an eye: If something happens in the twinkling of an eye, it happens very quickly.

In the zone: If you are in the zone, you are very focused on what you have to do.

In turn: This means one after the other. Example: She spoke to each of the guests in turn.

In your face: If someone is in your face, they are direct and confrontational.

In your sights: If you have someone or something in your sights, they are your target to beat.

Indian file: If people walk in Indian file, they walk in a line one behind the other.

Indian giver: An Indian giver gives something, then tries to take it back.

Indian summer: If there is a period of warmer weather in late autumn, it is an Indian summer.

Ins and outs: If you know the ins and outs of something, you know all the details.

Into each life some rain must fall: This means that bad or unfortunate things will happen to everyone at some time.

Into thin air: If something vanishes or disappears without trace, it vanishes into thin air; no-one knows where it has gone.

Iron fist: Someone who rules or controls something with an iron fist is in absolute control and tolerates no dissent. An iron fist in a velvet glove is used to describe someone who appears soft on the outside, but underneath is very har 'Mailed fist' is an alternative form.

Irons in the fire: A person who has a few irons in the fire has a number of things working to their advantage at the same time.

Is Saul also among the prophets?: It's a biblical idiom used when somebody known for something bad appears all of a sudden to be doing something very good.

It ain't over till the fat lady sings: This idiom means that until something has officially finished, the result is uncertain.

It cost an arm and a leg: If something costs an arm and a leg, it is very expensive indeed.

It cost the earth: If something costs the earth, it is very expensive indeed.

It never rains but it pours: 'It never rains but it pours' means that when things go wrong, they go very wrong.

It takes a village to raise a child: It takes many people to teach a child all that he or she should know.

It takes two to tango: This idiom is used to suggest that when things go wrong, both sides are involved and neither side is completely innocent.

It's an ill wind that blows no good: This is said when things have gone wrong; the idea being that when bad things happen, there can also be some positive results.

It's no use crying over spilt milk: This idiom means that getting upset after something has gone wrong is pointless; it can't be changed so it should be accepted.

It's not the size of the dog in fight, it's the size of the fight in the dog: Usually refering to a small dog attacking a larger animal, this means that fierceness is not necessarily a matter of physical size, but rather mental/psychological attitude.

It's not the size of the man in the fight, it's the size of the fight in the man: This idiom means that determination is often more important than size, strength, or ability.

It's your funeral: The other person has made a decision that you think is bad. However, it is their choice; it is their funeral.

Itch to: If you are itching to do something, you are very eager to do it.

Ivory tower: People who live in ivory towers are detached from the world around them.

J

Jack Frost: If everything has frozen in winter, then Jack Frost has visited.

Jack-of-all-trades: A jack-of-all-trades is someone that can do many different jobs.

Jam on your face: If you say that someone has jam on their face, they appear to be caught, embarrassed or found guilty.

Jam tomorrow: (UK) This idiom is used when people promise good things for the future that will never come.

Jane Doe: Jane Doe is a name given to an unidentified female who may be party to legal proceedings, or to an unidentified person in hospital, or dead. John Doe is the male equivalent.

Jekyll and Hyde: Someone who has a Jekyll and Hyde personality has a pleasant and a very unpleasant side to the character.

Jersey justice: (UK) Jersey justice is very severe justice.

Jet set: Very wealthy people who travel around the world to attend parties or functions are the jet set.

Jet-black: To emphasise just how black something is, such as someone's hair, we can call it jet-black.

Job's comforter: Someone who says they want to comfort, but actually discomforts people is a Job's comforter.

Jobs for the boys: Where people give jobs, contracts, etc, to their friends and associates, these are jobs for the boys.

Jockey for position: If a number of people want the same opportunity and are struggling to emerge as the most likely candidate, they are jockeying for position.

Jog my memory: If you jog someone's memory, you say words that will help someone trying to remember a thought, event, word, phrase, experience, etc.

John Doe: John Doe is a name given to an unidentified male who may be party to legal proceedings, or to an unidentified person in hospital, or dead. Jane Doe is the female equivalent.

John Q Public: (USA) John Q Public is the typical, average person.

Johnny on the spot: A person who is always available; ready, willing, and able to do what needs to be done.

Johnny-come-lately: A Johnny-come-lately is someone who has recently joined something or arrived somewhere, especially when they want to make changes that are not welcome.

Joined at the hip: If people are joined at the hip, they are very closely connected and think the same way.

Judge, jury and executioner: If someone is said to be the judge, jury, and executioner, it means they are in charge of every decision made, and they have the power to be rid of whomever they choose.

Juggle frogs: If you are juggling frogs, you are trying to do something very difficult.

Jump down someone's throat: If you jump down someone's throat, you criticise or chastise them severely.

Jump on the bandwagon: If people jump on the bandwagon, they get involved in something that has recently become very popular.

Jump the gun: If you jump the gun, you start doing something before the appropriate time.

Jump the shark: Said of a salient point in a television show or other activity at which the popularity thereof begins to wane: The Flintstones jump the shark when a man from outer space cam visit them. The expression derives fro episode of the television sitcom 'Happy D which Fonzie, clad in leather jacket and on water skis, jumps over a shark. That episode was widely seen as the beginning of the end for the formerly popular series.

Jump through hoops: If you are prepared to jump through hoops for someone, you are prepared to make great efforts and sacrifices for them.

Jump to a conclusion: If someone jumps to a conclusion, they evaluate or judge something without a sufficient examination of the facts.

Jumping Judas!: An expression of surprise or shock.

Jungle out there: If someone says that it is a jungle out there, they mean that the situation is dangerous and there are no rules.

K

Kangaroo court: When people take the law into their own hands and form courts that are not legal, these are known as kangaroo court.

Keen as mustard: (UK) If someone is very enthusiastic, they are as keen as mustard.

Keep abreast: If you keep abreast of things, you stay informed about developments.

Keep at bay: If you keep someone or something at bay, you maintain a safe distance from them.

Keep body and soul together: If you earn enough to cover your basic expenses, but nothing more than that, you earn enough to keep body and soul together.

Keep in touch: If you keep in touch with someone, you keep communicating with them even though you may live far apart.

Keep it on the Q T: If you keep something on the Q T, you keep it quiet or secret.

Keep it under your hat: If you keep something under your hat, you keep it secret.

Keep mum: If you keep mum about something, you keep quiet and don't tell anyone.

Keep posted: If you keep posted about something, you keep up-to-date with information and developments.

Keep someone at arm's length: If you keep someone or something at arm's length, you keep a safe distance away from them.

Keep someone on their toes: If you keep someone on their toes, you make sure that they concentrate on what they are supposed to do.

Keep the wolf at bay: If you keep the wolf at bay, you make enough money to avoid going hungry or falling heavily into debt.

Keep up with the Joneses: People who try to keep up with the Joneses are competitive about material possessions and always try to have the latest and best things.

Keep your ear to the ground: If you keep your ear to the ground, you try to keep informed about something, especially if there are rumours or uncertainties.

Keep your eye on the ball: If you keep your eye on the ball, you stay alert and pay close attention to what is happening.

Keep your eye on the prize: This means that you should keep your focus on achieving a positive end result.

Keep your eyes peeled: If you keep your eyes peeled, you stay alert or watchful.

Keep your fingers crossed: If you are keeping your fingers crossed, you are hoping for a positive outcome.

Keep your hair on: Keep your hair on is advice telling someone to keep calm and not to over-react or get angry.

Keep your head: If you keep your head, you stay calm in times of difficulty.

Keep your head above water: If you are just managing to survive financially, you are keeping your head above water.

Keep your nose clean: If someone is trying to keep their Nose Clean, they are trying to stay out of trouble by not getting involved in any sort of wrong-doing.

Keep your nose to the grindstone: If you keep your nose to the grindstone, you work hard and seriously.

Keep your options open: If someone's keeping their options open, they aren't going to restrict themselves or rule out any possible course of action.

Keep your pecker up: If someone tells you to keep your pecker up, they are telling you not to let your problems get on top of you and to try to be optimistic.

Keep your powder dry: If you keep your powder dry, you act cautiously so as not to damage your chances.

Keep your shirt on!: This idiom is used to tell someone to calm down.

Keep your wig on!: (UK) This idiom is used to tell someone to calm down.

Kettle of fish: A pretty or fine kettle of fish is a difficult problem or situation.

Kick a habit: If you kick a habit, you stop doing it.

Kick away the ladder: If someone kicks away the ladder, they remove something that was supporting or helping someone.

Kick in the teeth: Bad news or a sudden disappointment are a kick in the teeth.

Kick your heels: (UK) If you have to kick your heels, you are forced to wait for the result or outcome of something.

Kindred spirit: A kindred spirit is someone who feels and thinks the way you do.

King of the castle: The king of the castle is the person who is in charge of something or in a very comfortable position compared to their companions.

King's ransom: If something costs or is worth a king's ransom, it costs or is worth a lot of money.

Kiss something goodbye: If someone tells you that you can kiss something goodbye, you have no chance of getting or having it.

Kissing cousin: A kissing cousin is someone you ar related to, but not closely.

Kitchen-sink: (UK) Kitchen-sink drama deals ordinary people's lives.

Kith and kin: Your kith and kin are your family; your next of kin are close relations you nominate to deal with your affairs in the event of your death on a document, like a passport.

Knight in shining armour: A knight in shining armour is someone who saves you when you are in great trouble or danger.

Knit your brows: If you knit your brows, you frown or look worried.

Knock 'em dead: 'Knock 'em dead' is used as a way of wishing someone luck before they give a performance or have to appear before people, as in an interview, etc. ('em = them)

Knock on wood: This idiom is used to wish for good luck.

Knock something on the head: If you knock something on the head, you stop it or stop doing it.

Knock the pins from under someone: If someone knocks the pins from under you, they let you down.

Knock your block off: To punch someone in the face Eg: The next time you do something like that I'm going to "knock your block off".

Knock your socks off: If something knocks your socks off, it amazes and surprises you, usually in a positive way.

Know the ropes: Someone who is experienced and knows how the system works know the ropes.

Know where all the bodies are buried: Someone who by virtue of holding a position of trust with an organization for a long period of time has come to know many of the secrets that others in more powerful positions would rather be kept secret knows where the bodies are buried. An implication is that the person knowing these secrets will use that knowledge to secure something of value for him- or herself.

Know your onions: If someone is very well-informed about something, they know their onions.

Know your place: A person who knows their place doesn't try to impose themselves on others.

L

Labor of love: A labor of love is a project or task undertaking for the interest or pleasure in doing it rather than the reward, financial or otherwise.

Labour of love: A labour of love is a project or task undertaking for the interest or pleasure in doing it rather than the reward, financial or otherwise.

Lame duck: If something or someone is a lame duck, they are in trouble.

Land of nod: If someone has gone to the land of nod, they have fallen asleep or gone to bed.

Landslide victory: A landslide victory is a victory in an election by a very large margin.

Lap dog: A lap dog is a person who is eager to please another at the expense of his or her own needs in order to maintain a position of privilege or favor.

Lap of the gods: If something is in the lap of the gods, it is beyond our control and fate will decide the outcome.

Larger than life: If something is excessive or exaggerated, it is larger than life.

Last hurrah: If an elderly person does something special before they die, it is a last hurrah.

Last laugh: The person who has the last laugh ends up with the the advantage in a situation after some setbacks.

Last straw: The last straw is the final problem that makes someone lose their temper or the problem that finally brought about the collapse of something. It comes from an Arabic story, where a camel was loaded with straw until a single straw placed on the rest of the load broke its back.

Last-ditch: A last-ditch attempt is a desperate attempt that will probably fail anyway.

Laugh a minute: Someone who is a laugh a minute is very funny.

Laugh to see a pudding crawl: (UK) Someone who would laugh to see a pudding crawl is easily amused and will laugh at anything.

Laugh up your sleeve: If you laugh up your sleeve, you laugh at someone secretly.

Laughing stock: If someone becomes a laughing stock they do something so stupid or wrong that no one can take them seriously and people scorn and laugh at them.

Laughter is the best medicine: Laughing is often helpful for healing, especially emotional healing.

Law unto yourself: If somebody's a law unto themselves, they do what they believe is right regardless of what is generally accepted as correct.

Lay down the law: If someone lays down the law, they tell people what to do and are authoritarian.

Lead someone up the garden path: If someone leads you up the garden path, they deceive you, or give you false information that causes you to waste your time. 'Lead someone down the garden path' is also used.

Lead with the chin: If someone leads with their chin, they speak or behave without fear of the consequences.

Leave well alone: If you leave something well alone, you keep a safe distance from it, either physically or metaphorically.

Left hand doesn't know what the right hand is doing: If the left hand doesn't know what the right hand is doing, then communication within a company, organisation, group, etc, is so bad that people don't know what the others are doing.

Left to your own devices: If someone is left to their own devices, they are not controlled and can do what they want.

Left-handed compliment: A left-handed compliment is one that sounds like praise but has an insulting meaning.

Lesser of two evils: Something that is the lesser of two evils, is an unpleasant option, but not as bad as the other.

Let alone: This is used to emphasise how extre' something could be: 'We hadn't got the m to phone home, let alone stay in a hotel.' This emphasises the utter impossibility of staying in a hotel.

Let sleeping dogs lie: If someone is told to let sleeping dogs lie, it means that they shouldn't disturb a situation as it would result in trouble or complications.

Let the best be the enemy of the good: If the desire for an unattainable perfection stops someone from choosing good possibilities, they let the best be the enemy of the good.

Let the genie out of the bottle: If people let the genie out of the bottle, they let something bad happen that cannot be put right or controlled.

Let the grass grow round your feet: If you let the grass grow round your feet, you delay doing things instead of taking action.

Let's call it a day: This is used as a way of suggesting that it is time to stop working on something.

Letter of the law: If people interpret laws and regulations strictly, ignoring the ideas behind them, they follow the letter of the law.

Level playing field: If there's a level playing field everybody is treated equally.

Lie like a rug: If someone lies like a rug, they lie to the point where it becomes obvious that they're lying.

Life and limb: When people risk life and limb, they could be killed or suffer serious injuries.

Life is just a bowl of cherries: This idiom means that life is simple and pleasant.

Light bulb moment: A light bulb moment is when you have a sudden realisation about something, like the light bulbs used to indicate an idea in cartoons.

Light on your feet: If someone is light on their feet, they can move quickly and are agile.

Light years ahead: If you are light years ahead of others, you are a long way in front of them in terms of development, success, etc.

Lightning rod: Someone or something that attracts a lot of negative comment, often diverting attention from other problems, is a lightning rod.

Like a bat out of hell: This expression means extremely quickly.

Like a beached whale: Once a whale is on a beach, it cannot get back into the easily, so if you are completely stuck somewhere and can't get away, you are stranded like a beached whale.

Like a bear with a sore head: (UK) If someone's like a bear with a sore head, they complain a lot and are unhappy about something.

Like a bull at a gate: If you tackle a job very quickly, without any real thought about what you are doing, you are going at it like a bull at a gate.

Like a cat that got the cream: If someone looks very pleased with themselves and happy, they look like a cat that got the cream.

Like a duck to water: If someone has a natural talent for something and enjoys it, they take to it like a duck to water.

Like a fish needs a bicycle: If someone needs something like a Fish Needs a Bicycle, they do not need it at all, originally a feminist slogan: A woman needs a man like a fish needs a bicycle.

Like a headless chicken: If someone rushes about like a headless chicken, they move very fast all over the place, usually without thinking.

Like a kid in a candy store: If someone is like a kid in a candy store, they are very excited about something.

Like a rat deserting a sinking ship: If people leave a company because they know that it's about to have serious problems, or turn their back on a person about to be in a similar situation, they are said to be like rats deserting a sinking ship.

Like Chinese arithmetic: If something is complicated and hard to understand, it's like Chinese arithmetic.

Like clockwork: If something happens like clockwork, it happens at very regular times or intervals.

Like father, like son: This idiom is used when different generations of a family behave in the same way or have the same talents of defects.

Like giving a donkey strawberries: (UK) If something is like giving a donkey strawberries, people fail to appreciate its value.

Like it or lump it: When people say this, they mean that the person will have to accept the situation because it isn't going to change.

Like lambs to the slaughter: If somebody does something unpleasant without any resistance, they go like lambs to the slaughter.

Like no one's business: If I say my children are growing like no one's business, it means they're growing very quickly. See also 'Like the clappers' and 'Like there's no tomorrow'.

Like peas in a pod: If people or things are like peas in a pod, they look identical.

Like pulling teeth: If something if like pulling teeth, it is very difficult, especially if trying to extract information or to get a straight answer from someone.

Like taking candy from a baby: (USA) If something is like taking candy from a baby, it is very easy to do.

Like the back of your hand: If you know something like the back of your hand, you know it very well indeed.

Like the clappers: If something is going like the clappers, it is going very fast.

Like there's no tomorrow: If you do something like there's no tomorrow, you do it fast or energetically.

Like two peas in a pod: Things that are like two peas in a pod are very similar or identical,

Like watching sausage getting made: If something is like watching sausages getting made, unpleasant truths about it emerge that make it much less appealing. The idea is that if people watched sausages getting made, they would probably be less fond of them.

Like white on rice: (USA) If you do something lik white on rice, you do it very closely: When F found out I had front row tickets for the concert, he stuck to me like white on rice.

Like wildfire: If something happens or spreads like wildfire, it happens very quickly and intensely.

Lily-livered: Someone who is lily-livered is a coward.

Lines of communication: Lines of communication are the routes used to communicate by people or groups who are in conflict; a government might open lines of communication with terrorists if it wished to negotiate with them.

Lion's share: The lion's share of something is the biggest or best part.

Lip service: When people pay lip service to something, they express their respect, but they don't act on their words, so the respect is hollow and empty.

Little pitchers have big ears: (USA) This means that children hear more and understand the world around them better than many adults realise.

Little strokes fell great oaks: Meaning: even though something may seem impossible, if you break it up into small parts and take one step at a time, you will succeed.

Live high off the hog: If you are living high off the hog, you are living lavishly.

Live wire: A person who is very active, both mentally and physically, is a live wire.

Lo and behold: This phrase is used to express surprise.

Loan shark: A loan shark lends money at very high rates of interest.

Lock and load: This is a military term meaning "be ready and prepared".

Lock horns: When people lock horns, they argue or fight about something.

Lock, stock and barrel: This is an expressions that means 'everything'; if someone buys a company lock, stock and barrel, they buy absolutely everything to do with the company.

Long face: Someone with a long face is sad or depressed about something.

Long in the tooth: If someone is long in the tooth, they are a bit too old to do something.

Long shot: If something is a long shot, there is only a very small chance of success.

Long time no hear: The speaker could say this when they have not heard from a person, either through phone calls or emails for a long time.

Long time no see: 'Long time no see' means that the speaker has not seen that person for a long time.

Look after number 1: You are number one, so this idiom means that you should think about yourself first, rather than worrying about other people.

Look after the pennies and the pounds will look after themselves: (UK) If you look after the pennies, the pounds will look after themselves, meaning that if someone takes care not to waste small amounts of money, they will accumulate capital.

Look before you leap: This idiom means that you should think carefully about the possible results or consequences before doing something.

Look on the bright side: If you look on the bright side, you try to see things in an optimistic way, especially when something has gone wrong.

Look out for number one: If you look out for number one, you take care of yourself and your interests, rather than those of other people.

Look what the cat dragged in: This idiom is used when someone arrives somewhere looking a mess or flustered and bothered.

Loose cannon: A person who is very difficult to control and unpredictable is a loose cannon.

Lose the plot: If someone loses the plot, they have stopped being rational about something.

Lose your bottle: (UK) If someone loses their bottle, they lose the courage to do something.

Lose your lunch: (UK) If you lose your lunch, you vomit.

Lose your marbles: If someone has lost their marbles, they've gone mad.

Lose your shirt: If someone loses their shirt, they lose all their money through a bad investment, gambling, etc.

Love is blind: If you love someone, it doesn't matter what they look like. You will also overlook faults.

Low-hanging fruit: Low-hanging fruit are things that are easily achieved.

Lower than a snake's belly: Someone or something that is lower than a snake's belly is of a very low moral standing.

Lower than a snake's belly in a wagon rut: (USA) If someone or something is lower than a snake's belly in a wagon rut, they are of low moral standing because a snake's belly is low and if the snake is in a wagon rut, it is really low.

Lower the bar: If people change the standards required to make things easier, they lower the bar.

Lower your sights: If you lower your sights, you accept something that is less than you were hoping for.

Luck of the draw: To have the 'Luck of the draw' is to win something in a competition where the winner is chosen purely by chance.

M

Mad as a badger: If someone is as mad as a badger, they are crazy.

Mad as a bag of hammers: Someone who is as mad as a bag of hammers is crazy or stupid.

Mad as a cut snake: (USA) One who is mad as a cut snake has lost all sense of reason, is crazy, out of control.

Mad as a hornet: (USA) If someone is as mad as a hornet, they are very angry indeed.

Mad as a March hare: Someone who is excitable and unpredictable is as mad as a March hare.

Made in the shade: One has an easy time in life or in a given situation. Finding things working ' one's benefit.

Made of money: If you are made of money, you have a lot of money.

Mailed fist: Someone who rules or controls something with a mailed fist is in absolute control and tolerates no dissent. A mailed fist in a velvet glove is used to describe someone who appears soft on the outside, but underneath is very hard. 'Iron fist' is an alternative form.

Major league: Something major league is very important.

Make a better fist: If someone makes a better fist of doing something, they do a better job.

Make a clean breast: If someone makes a clean breast, they confess in full to something they have done.

Make a killing: If you make a killing, you do something that makes you a lot of money.

Make a meal: If someone makes a meal of something, they spend too long doing it or make it look more difficult than it really is.

Make a mint: If someone is making a mint, they are making a lot of money.

Make a monkey of someone: If you make a monkey of someone, you make them look foolish.

Make a mountain out of a molehill: If somebody makes a mountain out of a molehill, they exaggerate the importance or seriousness of a problem.

Make a pig's ear: If you make a pig's ear of something, you make a mess of it.

Make a pitch: If you make a pitch for something, you make a bid, offer or other attempt to get it.

Make a request: If you request something, or make a request, you are asking for something you want or need.

Make a song and dance: (UK) If someone makes a song and dance, they make an unecessary fuss about something unimportant.

Make an enquiry: If you make an enquiry, you ask for general information about something.

Make bets in a burning house: (USA) If people are making bets in a burning house, they are engaged in futile activity while serious problems around them are getting worse.

Make ends meet: If somebody finds it hard to make ends meet, they have problems living on the money they earn.

Make hay: If you make hay, or may hay while the sun shines, you take advantage of an opportunity as soon as it arises and do not waste time.

Make headway: If you make headway, you make progress.

Make your toes curl: If something makes your toes curl, it makes you feel very uncomfortable, shocked or embarrassed.

Man Friday: From 'Robinson Crusoe', a 'Man Friday' refers to an assistant or companion, usually a capable one. The common feminine equivalent is 'Girl Friday'.

Man of the cloth: A man of the cloth is a priest.

Man proposes, God disposes: Your fate lies in the hand of God.

Man upstairs: When people refer to the man upstairs, they are referring to God.

Man's best friend: This is an idiomatic term for dogs.

Man's man: A man's man is a man who does things enjoyed by men and is respected by other men.

Many a slip twixt cup and lip: There's many a slip twixt cup and lip means that many things can go wrong before something is achieved.

Many hands make light work: This idiom means that when everyone gets involved in something, the work gets done quickly.

Many happy returns: This expression is used to wish someone a happy birthday.

Many moons ago: A very long time ago.

March to the beat of your own drum: If people march to the beat of their own drum, they do things the way they want without taking other people into consideration.

Mark my words: Mark my words is an expression used to lend an air of seriousness to what the speaker is about to say when talking about the future. You often hear drunks say it before they deliver some particularly spurious nonsense.

Mark someone's card: If you mark someone's card, you correct them in a forceful and prompt manner when they say something wrong.

Marked man: A marked man is a person who is being targeted by people who want to do them harm or cause them trouble.

Meet your expectations: If something doesn't meet your expectations, it means that it wasn't as good as you had thought it was going to be; a disappointment.

Meet your Maker: If someone has gone to meet their Maker, they have died.

Meet your match: If you meet your match, you meet a person who is at least as good if not better than you are at something.

Megaphone diplomacy: If negotiations between countries or parties are held through press releases and announcements, this is megaphone diplomacy, aiming to force the other party into adopting a desired position.

Melt your heart: If something melts your heart, it affects you emotionally and you cannot control the feeling.

Melting pot: A melting pot is a place where people from many ethnicities and nationalities live together.

Memory like a sieve: If somebody can't retain things for long in his or her memory and quickly forgets, he or she has a memory like a sieve. A sieve has lots of tiny holes in it to let liquids out while keeping the solids inside.

Memory like an elephant: 'An elephant never forgets' is a saying, so if a person has a memory like an elephant, he or she has a very good memory indeed.

Mend fences: When people mend fences, they try to improve or restore relations that have beer damaged by disputes or arguments.

Mess with a bull, you get the horns: If you do something stupid or dangerous, you can get hurt.

Method in his madness: If there's method in someone's madness, they do things in a strange and unorthodox way, but manage to get results.

Mexican standoff: When there is a deadlock in strategy and neither side can do anything that will ensure victory, it's a Mexican standoff.

Mickey Mouse: If something is Mickey Mouse, it is intellectually trivial or not of a very high standard.

Midas touch: If someone has the Midas touch, they make a lot of money out of any scheme they try.

Middle of nowhere: If someone says that he/she is in the middle of nowhere, he/she means that he/she is not sure where he/she is.

Might and main: This means with all your effort and strength. As he failed in the previous exam,the student tried might and main to pass the next one.

Mighty oaks from little acorns grow: Big or great things start very small.

Millstone round your neck: A millstone around your neck is a problem that prevents you from doing what you want to do.

Mince words: If people mince words, or mince their words, they don't say what they really mean clearly.

Mind over matter: This idiom is used when someone uses their willpower to rise above adversity.

Mind the gap: Mind the gap is an instruction used on the Underground in the UK to warn passengers to be careful when leaving the tube or train as there is quite a distance between the train and the platform.

Mind your own beeswax: (USA) This idiom means that people should mind their own business and not interfere in other people's affairs.

Mind Your P's and Q's: If you are careful about the way you behave and are polite, you mind Your P's and Q's.

Mind your P's and Q's: This is used as a way of telling someone to be polite and behave well.

Mint condition: If something is in mint condition, it is in perfect condition.

Mom and pop: (USA) A mom and pop business is a small business, especially if it is run by members of a family. It can used in a wider sense to mean that something is small scale.

Monday morning quarterback: (USA) A Monday morning quarterback is someone who, with the benefit of hindsight, knows what should have been done in a situation.

Money to burn: If someone is very rich, they have money to burn.

Monkey business: If children get up to monkey business, they are behaving naughtily or mischievously. This is the same as 'monkeying around'.

Monkey see, monkey do: This idiom means that children will learn their behaviour by copying what they see happening around them.

Moot point: If something's a moot point, there's some disagreement about it: a debatable point. In the U.S., this expression usually means that there is no point in debating something, because it just doesn't matter. An example: If you are arguing over whether to go the beach or to the park, but you find out the car won't start and you can't go anywhere, then the destination is said to be a moot point.

Moral fibre: Moral fibre is the inner strength to do what you believe to be right in difficult situations Example: He lacked the moral fibre to be leader.

Moral high ground: If people have/take/claim/seize, etc, the moral high ground, they claim that their arguments, beliefs, etc, are morally superior to those being put forward by other people.

More heat than light: If a discussion generates more heat than light, it doesn't provide answers, but does make people angry.

More holes than Swiss cheese: If something has more holes than a Swiss cheese, it is incomplete,and lacks many parts.

More than meets the eye: If there is more than meets the eye to something, it is more complex or difficult than it appears.

More than one string to their bow: A person who has more than one string to their bow has different talents or skills to fall back on.

More than one way to skin a cat: When people say that there is more than one way to skin a cat, they mean that there are different ways of achieving the same thing.

More than you can shake a stick at: If you have more of something than you can shake a stick at, then you have a lot.

Mountain to climb: If you have a mountain to climb, you have to work hard or make a lot of progress to achieve something.

Move the goalposts: When people move the goalposts, they change the standards required for something to their advantage.

Mover and shaker: A person who is a mover and shaker is a highly respected, key figure in their particular area with a lot of influence and importance.

Much ado about nothing: If there's a lot of fuss about something trivial, there's much ado about nothing.

Muck or nettles: 'Muck or nettles' means 'all or nothing'.

Mud in the fire: The things that cannot be changed in the past that we usually forget about are mud in the fire.

Mud in your eye: This is a way of saying 'cheers' when you are about to drink something, normally alcohol.

Mud-slinging: If someone is mud-slinging, they are insulting someone and trying to damage tha' person's reputation.

Muddy the waters: If somebody muddies the wa he or she makes the situation more comp less clear.

Mum's the word: When people use this idiom, they mean that you should keep quiet about something and not tell other people.

Mummy's boy: A man who is still very dependent on his mother is a mummy's boy.

Murder will out: This idiom means that bad deeds can't be kept secret forever.

Murky waters: Where people are behaving in morally and ethically questionable ways, they are in murky waters.

Music to my ears: If something someone says is music to your ears, it is exactly what you had wanted to hear.

Mutton dressed as lamb: Mutton dressed as lamb is term for middle-aged or elderly people trying to look younger.

My dogs are barking: (USA) When someone says this, they mean that their feet are hurting.

My eye: This idiom is added to an adjective to show that you disagree with it: 'He's shy.' 'Shy my eye- he's just planning something secret.'

My foot!: This idiom is used to show that you do not believe what someone has just said.

My heart goes out to someone: If your heart goes out to someone, you feel genuine sympathy for them.

My way or the highway: This idiom is used to say that if people don't do what you say, they will have to leave or quit the project, etc.

N

Nail in the coffin: A nail in someone or something's

coffin is a problem or event that is a clear step towards an inevitable failure.

Nail-biter: If a game, election, contest, etc, is a nail-biter, it is exciting because the competitors are so close that it is impossible to predict the result.

Nature abhors a vacuum: This idiom is used to express the idea that empty or unfilled spaces are unnatural as they go against the laws of nature and physics.

Neck and neck: If two competitors or candidates, etc, are neck and neck, then they are very close and neither is clearly winning.

Neck of the woods: If someone talks about their neck of the woods, they mean the area where they live.

Need no introduction: Someone who is very famous and known to everyone needs no introduction.

Needle in a haystack: If trying to find something is like looking for a needle in a haystack, it means that it is very difficult, if not impossible to find among everything around it.

Neither fish nor fowl: Something or someone that is neither fish nor fowl doesn't really fit into any one group.

Neither here nor there: If something is neither here nor there, it is of very little importance.

Neither use nor ornament: Something that serves no purpose and is not aesthetically pleasing is neither use nor ornament.

Nerves of steel: If someone has nerves of steel, they don't get frightened when other people do.

Nervous Nellie: Someone excessively worried or apprehensive is a nervous Nellie.

Nest egg: If you have some money saved for the future, it is a nest egg.

Never a rose without the prick: This means that good things always have something bad as well; like the thorns on the stem of a rose.

Never darken my door again: This is a way of telling someone never to visit you again.

New blood: If something needs new blood, it has become stale and needs new ideas or people to invigorate it.

New brush sweeps clean: 'A new brush sweeps clean' means that someone with a new perspective can make great changes. However, the full version is 'a new brush sweeps clean, but an old brush knows the corners', which warns that experience is also a valuable thing. Sometimes 'broom' is used instead of 'brush'.

New sheriff in town: This is used when a new authority figure takes charge.

New York minute: (USA) If something happens in a New York minute, it happens very fast.

Newfangled: People who don't like new methods, technologies, etc, describe them as newfangled, which means new but not as good or nice as the old ones.

Nice as pie: If a person is nice as pie, they are surprisingly very kind and friendly. "After our argument, she was nice as pie!"

Nick of time: If you do something in the nick of time, you do it at the very last minute or second.

Nickel tour: (USA) If someone gives you a nickel tour, they show you around a place.

Night owl: A night owl is someone who goes to bed very late.

Ninth circle of hell: In Dante's Inferno, the ninth circle of hell is the centre where the worst punishments are found, so it is used idiomatically for something that couldn't get worse.

Nip and tuck: A close contest where neither opponent seems to be gaining the advantage.

Nip at the bit: If someone is nipping at the bit, they are anxious to get something done and don't want to wait.

Nip it in the bud: If you nip something in the bud, you deal with a problem when it is still small, before it can grow into something serious.

Nitty gritty: If people get down to the nitty gritty, they concentrate on the most important and serious issues.

No bed of roses: If something isn't a bed of roses, it is difficult.

No can do: No can do means that the speaker can't do whatever it is that has been asked of him or her.

No go: Something that will not work. 'A square peg in a round hole is a no go.'

No good deed goes unpunished: This means that life is unfair and people can do or try to do good things and still end up in a lot of trouble.

No great shakes: If someone is no great shakes at something, they are not very good at it.

No harm, no foul: There's no problem when no harm or damage is done, such as the time my sister-in-law stole the name we'd chosen for a boy and we both ended up having girls.

No laughing matter: Something that is no laughing matter is very serious.

No love lost: If there is no love lost between two people they have a strong enmity towards or hate for the other and make no effort to conceal it.

No pain, no gain: Achievements require some sort of sacrifice.

No quarter: This means without mercy. We can say no quarter given or asked.

No question: This idiom means that something is certain or definite.

No questions asked: If something is to be done and no questions asked, then it doesn't matter what methods are used or what rules are broken to ensure that it gets done.

No skin off my nose: If something's no skin off your nose, it doesn't affect or bother you at all.

No smoke without fire: This idiom means that when people suspect something, there is normally a good reason for the suspicion, even if there is no concrete evidence.

No spine: If someone has no spine, they lack courage or are cowardly.

No spring chicken: If someone is no spring chicken, they are not young.

No strings attached: If something has no strings attached, there are no obligations or requirements involved.

No time for: If you have no time for an activity, you have absolutely no desire to spend or waste any time doing it. You can have no time for people, too.

No time like the present: If people say that there's no time like the present , they believe that it is far better to do something now than to leave it for later, in which case it might never get done.

No time to lose: If there's no time to lose, then it's time to get started otherwise it won't be finished on time.

No use to man or beast: If something or someone is no use to man or beast, they it or they are utterly useless.

Nod's as good as a wink: (UK) 'A nod's as good as a wink' is a way of saying you have understood somethin that someone has said, even though it was not said directly. The full phrase is 'a nod's as good as a wink to a blind horse'.

Noddy work: (UK) Unimportant or very simple tasks are noddy work.

None so blind as those who will not see: This idiom is used when people refuse to accept facts presented to them.

Nosy parker: (UK) A nosy parker is someone who is excessively interested in other people's lives.

Not a snowball's chance in hell: There is absolutely no possibility of something hapening if there's not a snowball's chance in hell.

Not all there: If someone isn't all there, they are a little bit stupid or crazy.

Not bat an eye: If someone doesn't bat an eye, they do not react when other people normally would.

Not born yesterday: When someone says that they weren't born yesterday, they mean that they are not naive or easily fooled.

Not cricket: (UK) If something is not cricket, it is unfair.

Not enough room to swing a cat: If a room is very small, you can say that there isn't enough room to swing a cat in it.

Not give a monkey's: (UK) If you couldn't give a monkey's about something, you don't care at all about it.

Not have the heart: If you don't have the heart to do something, you don't have the strength or courage to do something.

Not much cop: Describing a film or something as not much cop is a way of saying that you didn't think much of it.

Not my cup of tea: If something is not your cup of tea, you don't like it very much.

Not on my watch: Someone distancing themselves from a situation could say that it is not on their watch.

Not our bag: If something is not your bag, it is not really suitable for your needs or you don't like it much.

Not the only pebble on the beach: If something is not the only pebble on the beach, there are other possibilities or alternatives.

Nuts and bolts: The nuts and bolts are the most essential components of something.

Nutty as a fruitcake Someone who's nutty as a fruitcake is irrational or crazy.

O

Object lesson: An object lesson serves as a warning to others.

Odds and ends L Odds and ends are small, remnant articles and things- the same as 'bits and bobs'.

Off colour: If someone looks off colour/color, they look ill.

Off the scale: If something goes off the scale, it far exceeds the normal standards, good or bad, for something.

Off the shelf: If a product is off the shelf, it can be used straightaway without any setting-up.

Off the top of your head: If you say something off the top of your head, you don't think about it beforehand.

Off the track: If something puts or throws you off your track, it distracts you or keeps you from achieving what you want.

Off the wall: Something that is off the wall is unconventional.

Off-hand: Off-hand means without preparation. People say that they don't know the answer off-hand, meaning that they don't know it at that time.

Oh, my goodness!: An expression of surprise.

Old chestnut: An old chestnut is something that has been repeated so many times that it has lost its impact.

Olive branch: If you hold out or offer an olive branch, you make a gesture to indicate that you want peace.

On a fishing expedition: If someone is on a fishing expedition, they are trying to get information, often using incorrect or improper ways to find things out.

On good terms: If people are on good terms, they have a good relationship.

On the ball: If someone's on the ball, they are well-informed and know what's going on in their area of responsibility or interest.

On the carpet: When you are called to the bosses office (since supposedly, they are the only ones who have carpet) and its definitely not for a good reason, i.e., you are in trouble, something has not gone according to plan and either maybe you are responsible and/or have some explaining to do.

On the case: If someone is on the case, they are dealing with a problem.

On the flip side: On the reverse or the other side

On the fly: If you do things on the fly, you do things without preparation, responding to events as they happen.

On the ground: Events on the ground are where things are actually happening, not at a distance.

On the lam: If someone is on the lam, they are hiding from the police or authorities, especially to avoid arrest or prison.

On the level: If someone is honest and trustworthy, they are on the level.

On the line: If somebody's job is on the line, they stand a very good chance of losing it.

On the nose: This means right on time.

On the rebound: If someone is on the rebound, their relationship has recently ended and they are emotionally unstable.

On the same page: If people are on the same page, they have the same information and are thinking the same way.

On the same wavelength: If people are on the same wavelength, they have the same ideas and opinions about something.

On the wagon: If someone is on the wagon, they have stopped drinking alcohol.

On your soapbox: If someone is up on their soapbox about something, they are very overtly and verbally passionate about the topic.

One bad apple: The full form of this proverb is 'one bad apple spoils the barrel', meaning that a bad person, policy, etc, can ruin everything around it.

One fell swoop: If something is done at one fell swoop, it is done in a single period of activity, usually swiftly and ruthlessly.

Open old sores: When a sore is almost healed, and if a person rips or tears it open, it is way of preventing the healing process and further aggravating the pain. This phrase, metaphorically suggests, to revive or reopen a quarrel or enmity which was almost forgotten.

Out of my league: If someone or something is out of your league, you aren't good enough or rich enough, etc, for it or them.

Out of pocket: If you are out of pocket on a deal, you have lost money.

Out of sight, out of mind: Out of sight, out of mind is used to suggest that someone will not think or worry about something if it isn't directly visible or available to them.

Out of the frying pan, into the fire: If you get out of one problem, but find yourself in a worse situation, you are out of the frying pan, into the fire.

Out of the gate running: If someone comes out of the gate running, they start something at a fast pace, without any build-up.

Out of this world: If something is out of this world, it is fantastic.

Out of your hair: If you get someone out of your hair, you get them to stop bothering or annoying you.

Out of your mind: If someone is out of the mind, they are so emotional about something that they are no longer rational.

Out of your own pocket: If someone does something out of their own pocket, they pay all the expenses involved.

Out on a limb: If somebody's out on a limb, they are in a very exposed position and could get into difficulties.

Out to lunch: If someone's out to lunch, they are crazy or out of touch.

Out-and-out: This means complete or total; an out-and-out lie is completey false.

Over a barrel: If someone has you over a barrel, they have you in a position where you have no choice but to accept what they want.

Over and over: If something happens over and over, it happens repeatedly.

Over my dead body: If you say that something will happen over your dead body, you will not let it happen.

Over the counter: Medicines and drugs that can be sold without a doctor's prescription are sold over the counter.

Over the hill: If someone is over the hill they have reached an age at which they can longer perform as well as they used to.

Over the moon: If you are over the moon about something, you are overjoyed.

Over the top: If something is over the top, it is excessive or unnecessary. It refers to the moment a soldier leaves the trenches.

Over your head: If something is over your head, or goes over your head, it is too complex or difficult for you to understand.

P

Pain in the neck: If someone is very annoying and always disturbing you, they are a pain in the neck. Pain in the butt, or pain in the ass (USA), and Pain in the arse (UK) are less polite alternative forms.

Pass the hat: If you pass the hat, you ask a people in a group to give money.

Pen is mightier than the sword: The idiom 'the pen is mightier than the sword' means that words and communication are more powerful than wars and fighting.

Penny pincher: A penny pincher is a mean person or who is very frugal.

Perfidious Albion: England is known to some as perfidious Albion, implying that it is not trustworthy in its dealings with foreigners.

Pick up the tab: A person who pays for everyone picks up the tab.

Pick-up game: (USA) A pick-up game is something unplanned where people respond to events as they happen.

Picture perfect: When something is exactly as it should be it is said to be picture perfect.

Pie in the sky: If an idea or scheme is pie in the sky, it is utterly impractical.

Piece of cake: If something is a piece of cake, it is really easy.

Pieces of the same cake: Pieces of the same cake are things that have the same characteristics or qualities.

Pig in a poke: If someone buys a pig in a poke, they buy something without checking the condition it was in, usually finding out later that it was defective.

Pigs might fly: If you think something will never happen or succeed, you can say that 'pigs might fly' (or 'pigs can fly' and 'pigs will fly'- the idiom is used in many forms)

Pin down with a label: If you pin someone down with a label, you characterise them, often meant negatively as the label is restrictive.

Plain as the nose on your face: If something is as plain as the nose on your face, it is very clear and obvious.

Plain Jane: A plain Jane is a woman who isn't particularly attractive.

Plain sailing: If something is relatively easy and there are no problems doing it, it is plain sailing.

Play for keeps: If you are playing for keeps, you take things very seriously and the outcome is very important to you; it is not a mere game.

Play hardball: If someone plays hardball, they are very aggressive in trying to achieve their aim.

Play the field: Someone who plays the field has sexual relationships with many people.

Play the fool: If someone plays the fool, they behave in a silly way to make people laugh.

Play with fire: If people take foolish risks, they are playing with fire.

Playing to the gallery: If someone plays to the gallery, they say or do things that will make them popular, but which are not the right things to do.

Politically correct: Things or people that are politically correct use language that will not cause offence.

Pot calling the kettle black: If someone hypocritically criticises a person for something that they themselves do, then it is a case of the pot calling the kettle black.

Pot-luck: If you take pot-luck, you take whatever happens to be available at the time.

Pound of flesh: If someone wants their pound of flesh, the force someone to pay or give back something owed, even though they don't need it and it will cause the other person a lot of difficulty.

Practical joke: A practical joke is a trick played on someone that is meant to be funny for people watching, though normally embarrassing for the person being tricked.

Preaching to the choir: If someone preaches to the choir, they talking about a subject or issue with which their audience already agrees.

Presence of mind: If someone behaves calmly and rationally in difficult circumstances, they show presence of mind.

Proclaim it from the rooftops: If something is proclaimed from the rooftops, it is made as widely known and as public as possible.

Proud as a peacock: Someone who is as proud as a peacock is excessively proud.

Pull a rabbit out of your hat: If you pull a rabbit out of a hat, you do something that no one was expecting.

Pull in the reins: When you pull in the reins, you slow down or stop something that has been a bit out of control.

Pull out all the stops: If you pull out all the stops, you do everything you possibly can to achieve the result you want.

Pull rank: A person of higher position or in authority pulls rank, he or she exercises his/her authority, generally ending any discussion and ignoring other people's views.

Pull strings: If you pull strings, you use contacts you have got to help you get what you want.

Pull the fat from the fire: If you pull the fat from the fire, you help someone in a difficult situation.

Pull the trigger: The person who pulls the trigger is the one who does the action that closes or finishes something.

Pull the wool over someone's eyes: If you pull the wool over someone's eyes, you deceive or cheat them.

Pull up your socks: If you aren't satisfied with someone and want them to do better, you can tell them to pull up their socks.

Put a bug in your ear: If you put a bug in someone's ear, you give him or her a reminder or suggestion relating to a future event.

Put a cork in it!: This is a way of telling someone to be quiet.

Put a sock in it: If someone tells you to put a sock in it, they are telling you to shut up.

Put all your eggs in one basket: If you put all your eggs in one basket, you risk everything on a single opportunity which, like eggs breaking, could go wrong.

Put it on the cuff: If you put something on the cuff, you will take it now and pay for it later.

Put lipstick on a pig: If people put lipstick on a pig, they make superficial or cosmetic changes, hoping that it will make the product more attractive.

Put on airs: If someone puts on airs, they pretend to be grander and more important than they really are.

Put or get someone's back up: If you put or get someone's back up, you annoy them.

Put some dirt on it: This means that when you get hurt, you should rub it off or shake it off and you'll be ok.

Put your thumb on the scales: If you put your thumb on the scales, you try to influence the result of something in your favour.

Pyrrhic victory: A Pyrrhic victory is one that causes the victor to suffer so much to achieve it that it isn't worth winning.

Q

Queen bee: The queen bee is a woman who holds the most important position in a place.

Queen of Hearts: A woman who is pre-eminent in her area is a Queen of Hearts.

Queer Street: If someone is in a lot of trouble, especially financial, they are in Queer Street.

Queer your pitch: If someone queers your pitch, they interfere in your affairs and spoil things.

Question of time: If something's a question of time, it's certain to happen, though we don't know exactly when.

Queue jumping: Someone who goes to the front of a queue instead of waiting is jumping the queue.

Quick as a flash: If something happens quick as a flash, it happens very fast indeed.

Quiet as a cat: If somebody is as quiet as a cat they make as little noise as possible and try to be unnoticeable.

R

Rack and ruin: If something or someone goes to rack and ruin, they are utterly destroyed or wrecked.

Rack your brain

If you rack your brain, you think very hard when trying to remember something.

Rack your brain: If you rack your brain, you think hard, especially when trying to remember something or find a solution.

Rags to riches: Someone who starts life very poor and becomes rich goes from rags to riches.

Rain on your parade: If someone rains on your parade, they ruin your pleasure or your plans.

Raining cats and dogs: When it is raining cats and dogs, it is raining very heavily.

Rainy day: If you save something, especially money, for a rainy day, you save it for some possible problem or trouble in the future.

Raise eyebrows: If something raises eyebrows, it shocks or surprises people.

Real deal: If something is the real deal, it is genuine and good.

Real McCoy: Something that's the real McCoy is the genuine article, not a fake.

Real plum: A real plum is a good opportunity.

Real trooper: A real trooper is someone who will fight for what they believe in and doesn't give up easily.

Recharge your batteries: If you recharge your batteries, you do something to regain your energy after working hard for a long time.

Recipe for disaster: A recipe for disaster is a mixture of people and events that could only possibly result in trouble.

Red carpet: If you give someone the red-carpet treatment, you give them a special welcome to show that you think they are important. You can roll out the red carpet, too.

Red herring: If something is a distraction from the real issues, it is a red herring.

Reds under the bed: An ironic allusion to the obsession some people have that there are reds (communists) everywhere plotting violent revolution.

Reduce to ashes: If something is reduced to ashes, it is destroyed or made useless. His infidelities reduced their relationship to ashes.

Reinvent the wheel: If someone reinvents the wheel, they waste their time doing something that has already been done by other people, when they could be doing something more worthwhile.

Renaissance man: A Renaissance man is a person who is talented in a number of different areas, especially when their talents include both the sciences and the arts.

Rest on your laurels: If someone rests on their laurels, they rely on their past achievements, rather than trying to achieve things now.

Ride with the tide: If you ride with the tide, you accept the majority decision.

Right as rain: If things are right as rain, then everything is going well in your life.

Right out of the blocks: This means immediately; at the very beginning. It describes a sprinter blasting out of the starting blocks at the beginning of a short distance race (e.g., 100-yard dash, 50-yard dash).

Right up my alley: If something is right up your alley, it suits you perfectly.

Ringside seat: If you have a ringside seat, you can observe something from a very close and clear position.

Rip van Winkle: Rip van Winkle is a character in a story who slept for twenty years, so if someone is a Rip van Winkle, they are behind the times and out of touch with what's happening now.

Rise from the ashes: If something rises from the ashes, it recovers after a serious failure.

Road to Damascus: If someone has a great and sudden change in their ideas or beliefs, then this is a road to Damascus change, after the conversion of Saint Paul to Christianity while heading to Damascus to persecute Christians.

Rob Peter to pay Paul: If you rob Peter to pay Paul, you try to solve one problem, but create another in doing so, often through short-term planning.

Rock the boat: If you rock the boat, you destabilise a situation by making trouble. It is often used as advice; 'Don't rock the boat'.

Rocket science: If something is not rocket science, it is not very complicated or difficult to understand. This idiom is normally used in the negative.

Roll out the red carpet: If you roll out the red carpet, you treat someone in a special way, especially when welcoming them.

Roll with the punches: If you roll with the punches, you are flexible and able to adapt to difficult circumstances.

Rooted to the spot: If someone is rooted to the spot, they canot move, either physically or they cannot think their way out of a problem.

Rose-colored glasses: If people see things through rose-colored (coloured) glasses, they see them in a more positive light than they really are.

Rough end of the stick: To get the rough end of the stick is to be treated unfairly or to come off worse than the other party in a transaction, situation or relationship.

Rub shoulders: If you rub shoulders with people, you meet and spend time with them, especially when they are powerful or famous.

Ruffle a few feathers: If you ruffle a few feathers, you annoy some people when making changes or improvements.

Run rings around someone: If you run rings around someone, you are so much better than them that they have no chance of keeping up with you.

Runs in the family: If a characteristic runs in the family, it can clearly be seen members of different generations. A hereditary illness that is passed from one generation to the next also runs in the family.

Russian roulette: If people take a dangerous and unnecessary risk, they are playing Russian roulette.

Rusty needle: When something is described as a rusty needle, it is badly damaged but still works, or if someone very is sick or tired but still manages to do things at a fairly good level. An alternative form is "a tarnished needle".

S

Sacred cow: Something that is a sacred cow is held in such respect that it cannot be criticised or attacked.

Safe and sound: If you arrive safe and sound, then nothing has harmed you on your way.

Safe bet: A proposition that is a safe bet doesn't have any risks attached.

Safe pair of hands: A person who can be trusted to do something without causing any trouble is a safe pair of hands.

Safety in numbers: If a lot of people do something risky at the same time, the risk is reduced because there is safety in numbers.

Salty dog: A salty dog is an experienced sailor.

Same old, same old: When nothing changes, it's the same old, same old.

Save face: If someone saves face, they manage to protect their reputation.

Save someone's bacon: If something saves your bacon, it saves your life or rescues you from a desperate situation. People can also save your bacon.

Say when: People say this when pouring a drink as a way of telling you to tell them when there's enough in your glass.

Scare the daylights out of someone: If you scare the daylights out of someone, you terrify them.

Scarlet woman: This idiom is used as a pejorative term for a sexually promiscuous woman, especially an adulteress.

Scotch Mist: The phrase 'Scotch mist' is used humorously to refer to something that is hard to find or doesn't exist - something imagined.

Seamy side: The seamy side of something is the unpleasant or sordid aspect it has.

See red: If someone sees red, they become very angry about something.

See the elephant: If you see the elephant, you experience much more than you wish to; it is often used when a soldier goes into a warzone for the first time.

See you later: A casual way of saying to friends I'll see you again, sometime, - this is often abbreviated to 'Later' or 'Laters' as an alternative way of saying goodbye.

Seeing is believing: This idiom means that people can only really believe what they experience personally.

Seen better days: If something's seen better days, it has aged badly and visibly compared to when it was new. The phrase can also be used to describe people.

Sell your soul: If someone sells their soul, their betray the most precious beliefs.

Send someone packing: If you send someone packing, you send them away, normally when they want something from you.

Separate the sheep from the goats: If you separate the sheep from the goats, you sort out the good from the bad.

Set the Thames on fire: If you do something remarkable, you set the Thames on fire, though this expression is used in the negative; someone who is dull or undistiguished will never set the Thames on fire.

Seventh heaven: If you are in seventh heaven, you are extremely happy.

Shake a leg: If you shake a leg, you are out of bed and active. It can be used to tell someone to hurry up.

Sharp cookie: Someone who isn't easily deceived or fooled is a sharp cookie.

Shed light: If you shed light on something, you make it clearer and easier to understand.

Shoot down in flames: If someone demolishes your argument, it (and you) have been shot down in flames.

Shoot from the hip: Someone who shoots from the hip talks very directly or insensitively without thinking beforehand.

Shoot the breeze: When you shoot the breeze, you chat in a relaxed way.

Short shrift: If somebody gives you short shrift, they treat you rudely and brusquely, showing no interest or sympathy.

Short-change: If you are short-changed, someone cheats you of money or doesn't give you full value for something.

Show someone a clean pair of heels: If you show someone a clean pair of heels, you run faster than them when they are chasing you.

Sick as a dog: If somebody's as sick as a dog, they throw up (=vomit) violently.

Sick as a parrot: If someone's sick as a parrot about something, they are unhappy, disappointed or depressed about it.

Sight to behold: If something is a sight to behold, it means that seeing it is in some way special, either spectacularly beautiful or, equally, incredibly ugly or revolting, etc.

Silly season: The silly season is midsummer when Parliament is closed and nothing much is happening that is newsworthy, which reduces the press to reporting trivial and stupid stories.

Silver surfer: A silver surfer is an elderly person who uses the internet.

Since time immemorial: If something has happened since time immemorial, it's been going on for such a long time that nobody can remember a time without it.

Sing for your supper: If you have to sing for your supper, you have to work to get the pay or reward you need or want.

Slow boat to China: This idiom is used to describe something that is very slow and takes a long time.

Smack in the face: If something is a smack in the face, it is a shock, usually one that impedes progress.

Smarty pants: A smarty pants is someone who displays the intelligence in an annoying way.

Smoking gun: A smoking gun is definitive proof of someone's guilt.

Some other time: If somebody says they'll do something some other time, they mean at some indefinite time in the future, possibly never, but they certainly don't want to feel obliged to fix a specific time or date.

Sow the seeds: When people sow the seeds, they start something that will have a much greater impact in the future.

Speak with a forked tongue: To say one thing and mean another, to lie, to be two-faced

Spice of life: The spice of life is something that makes it feel worth living.

Spin a yarn: If someone spins a yarn, they tell a story, usually a long or fanciful one.

Spirit of the law: The spirit of the law is the idea or ideas that the people who made the law wanted to have effect.

Spit it out: People say this when someone has something to say but is too embarrassed, shy, etc, to say it.

Spring to mind: If something springs to mind, it appears suddenly and unexpectedly in your thoughts.

Spur of the moment: If you do something on the spur of the moment, you do it because you felt like it at that time, without any planning or preparation.

Squared away: Being prepared or ready for business or tasks at hand. Having the proper knowledge, skill and equipment to handle your assignment or station. 'He is a great addition to the squad; he is squared away.'

Stalking horse: A stalking horse is a strategy or something used to conceal your intentions. It is often used where someone put themselves forwards as a candidate to divide opponents or to hide the real candidate.

Stick out like a sore thumb: If something sticks or stands out like a sore thumb, it is clearly and obviously different from the things that are around it.

Stick to your guns: If you stick to your guns, you keep your position even though people attack or criticise you.

Stick-in-the-mud: A stick-in-the-mud is someone who doesn't like change and wants things to stay the same.

Stick-in-the-mud: A stick-in-the-mud is a person who is old-fashioned, does not want to change the way they do things or innovate.

Succeed in the clutch: If you succeed in the clutch, you perform at a crucial time; it is particularly used in sports for the decisive moments of the game. The opposite is 'fail in the clutch.'

Sunday driver: A Sunday driver drives very slowly and makes unexpected manoeuvres.

Sweat blood: If you sweat blood, you make an extraordinary effort to achieve something.

Swings and roundabouts: If something's swings and roundabouts, it has about as many disadvantages as it has advantages.

T

Tables are turned: When the tables are turned, the situation has changed giving the advantage to the party who had previously been at a disadvantage.

Tackle an issue: If you tackle an issue or problem, you resolve or deal with it.

Take a hike: This is a way of telling someone to get out.

Take a raincheck: If you take a rain check, you decline an offer now, suggesting you will accept it later.

Take guts: If something takes guts, it requires courage in the face of danger or great risk. It takes guts for firemen to enter a burning building to save someone.

Take someone to task: If you take someone to task, you scold them for something they have done wrong.

Take the chair: If you take the chair, your become the chairman or chairwoman of a committee, etc.

Take the fall: If you tall the fall, you accept the blame and possibly the punishment for another's wrongdoing, with the implication that the true culprit, for political or other reasons, cannot be exposed as guilty.

Take the plunge: If you take the plunge, you decide to do something or commit yourself even though you know there is an element of risk involved.

Take the rough with the smooth: People say that you have to take the rough with the smooth, meaning that you have to be prepared to accept the disadvantages as well of the advantages of something.

Take to your heels: If you take to your heels, you run away.

Take up the torch: If you take up the torch, you take on a challenge or responsibility, usually when someone else retires, or leaves an organisation, etc.

Take your breath away: If something takes your breath away, it astonishes or surprises you.

Take your eye off the ball: If someone takes their eye off the ball, they don't concentrate on something important that they should be looking at.

Take your hat off: If you say that you take your hat off to someone, you are showing your respect or admiration.

Take your hat off to somebody: If you take your hat off to someone, you acknowledge that they have done something exceptional or otherwise deserve your respect.

Talk of the town: When everybody is talking about particular people and events, they are he talk of the town.

Talk turkey: When people talk turkey, they discuss something frankly.

Tar baby: A tar baby is a problem that gets worse when people try to sort it out.

Teeny-weeny: If something is teensy-weensy, it is very small indeed.

Tempest in a teapot: If people exaggerate the seriousness of a situation or problem, they are making a tempest in a teapot.

The be all and end all: The phrase 'The be all and end all' means that a something is the final, or ultimate outcome or result of a situation or event.

The common weal: If something is done for the common weal, it is done in the interests and for the benefit of the majority or the general public.

The grass is always greener: This idiom means that what other people have or do looks preferable to our life. The complete phrase is 'The grass is always greener on the other side of the fence'.

The sands of time: The sands of time is an idiom meaning that time runs out either through something reaching an end or through a person's death. It comes from the sand used in hourglasses, an ancient way of measuring time.

The short straw: If you take the short straw, you lose a selection process, which means that you have to do something unpleasant.

Thick as thieves: If people are thick as thieves, they are very close friends who have no secrets from each other.

Thick-skinned: If a person is thick-skinned, they are not affected by criticism.

Thin as a rake: A rake is a garden tool with a long, thin, wooden handle, so someone very thin is thin as a rake.

Thin line: If there's a thin line between things, it's hard to distinguish them- there's a thin line between love and hate.

Thin-skinned: If somebody is thin-skinned, they are very sensitive to any sort of criticism.

Third degree: If someone is given the third degree, they are put under a great deal of pressure and intimidation to force them to tell the truth about something.

Third rail: The third rail of something is dangerous to alter or change. Originally, the third rail is the one carrying the electricity for a train.

Tickled pink: If you are very pleased about something, you are tickled pink.

To a fault: If something does something to a fault, they do it excessively. So someone who is generous to a fault is too generous.

To a man: If a group of people does, believes, thinks, etc, something to a man, then they all do it.

To a T: If something is done to a T, it is done perfectly.

To all intents and purposes: This means in all the most important ways.

To be as thick as two bricks: Someone who is as thick as two bricks is really stupid.

Top dog: The most important or influential person is the top dog.

Top notch: If something is top notch, it's excellent, of the highest quality or standard.

Touch and go: If something is touch and go, the result is uncertain and could be good or bad.

Touch base: If you touch base with someone, you contact them.

Touch wood: This idiom is used to wish for good luck.

Touch-and-go: If something is touch-and-go, it is very uncertain; if someone is ill and may well die, then it is touch-and-go.

Tough as old boots: Something or someone that is as tough as old boots is strong and resilient.

Tough cookie: A tough cookie is a person who will do everything necessary to achieve what they want.

Turn-up for the books: A turn-up for the books is an unexpected or surprising event.

U

U-turn: If a government changes its position radically on an issue, especially when they have promised not to do so, this is a U-turn.

Uncharted waters: If you're in uncharted waters, you are in a situation that is unfamiliar to you, that you have no experience of and don't know what might happen.

Under a cloud: If someone is suspected of having done something wrong, they are under a cloud.

Under a flag of convenience: If a ship sails under a flag of convenience, it is registered in a country where taxes, etc, are lower than in the country it comes from, so if someone does something under a flag of convenience, they attempt to avoid regulations and taxes by a similar means.

Under false colours: If someone does something under false colours/colors, they pretend to be something they are not in order to deceive people so that they can succeed.

Under fire: If someone is being attacked and cricitised heavily, they are under fire.

Under lock and key: If something is under lock and key, it is stored very securely.

Under someone's heel: If you are under someone's heel, they have complete control over you.

Under the radar: If something slips under the radar, it isn't detected or noticed.

Under the table: Bribes or illegal payments are often described as money under the table.

Under the weather: If you are feeling a bit ill, sad or lack energy, you are under the weather.

Under your belt: If you have something under your belt, you have already achieved or experienced it and it will probably be of benefit to you in the future.

Under your breath: If you say something under your breath, you whisper or say it very quietly.

Under your nose: If something happens right in front of you, especially if it is surprising or audacious, it happens under your nose.

Under your skin: If someone gets under your skin, they really annoy you.

Under your thumb: Someone who is manipulated or controlled by another person is under his or her thumb.

Uneasy lies the head that wears the crown: This means that people with serious responsibilities have a heavy burden.

Up the wooden hill: When you go up the wooden hill, you go up the stairs to bed.

Upper hand: If you have the upper hand, you have the advantage.

V

Vale of tears: This vale of tears is the world and the suffering that life brings.

Velvet glove: This idiom is used to describe a person who appears gentle, but is determined and inflexible underneath.

Vent your spleen: If someone vents their spleen, they release all their anger about something.

Vicious circle: A vicious circle is a sequence of events that make each other worse- someone drinks because they are unhappy at work, then loses their job... 'Vicious cycle' is also used.

Virgin territory: If something is virgin territory, it hasn't been explored before.

Volte-face: If you do a volte-face on something, you make a sudden and complete change in your stance or position over an issue.

W

Wag the dog: To 'wag the dog' means to purposely

divert attention from what would otherwise be of greater importance, to something else of lesser significance. By doing so, the lesser-significant event is catapulted into the limelight, drowning proper attention to what was originally the more important issue.The expression comes from the saying that 'a dog is smarter than its tail', but if the tail were smarter, then the tail would 'wag the dog'. The expression 'wag the dog' was elaborately used as theme of the movie. 'Wag the Dog', a 1997 film starring Robert de Niro and Dustin Hoffman, produced and directed by Barry Levinson.

Wait for a raindrop in the drought: When someone is waiting for a raindrop in the drought, they are waiting or hoping for something that is extremely unlikely to happen.

Waiting in the wings: If someone is waiting in the wings, or in the wings, they are in the background, but nearby, ready to act on short notice.

Wake up and smell the coffee: When someone doesn't realise what is really happening or is not paying enough attention to events around them, you can tell them to wake up and smell the coffee.

Wake-up call: A wake-up call is a warning of a threat or a challenge, especially when it means that people will have to change their behaviour to meet it.

Walk a fine line: If you have to walk a fine line, you have to be very careful not to annoy or anger people or groups that are competing.

Walk a mile in my shoes: This idiom means that you should try to understand someone before criticising them.

Walk a tightrope: If you walk a tightrope, you have to be very careful not to annoy or anger people who could become enemies.

Walk in the park: An undertaking that is easy is a walk in the park. The opposite is also true - "no walk in the park".

Walk on eggshells: If you have to walk on eggshells when with someone, you have to be very careful because they get angry or offended very easily.

Walk the green mile: Someone or something that is walking the green mile is heading towards the inevitable.

Walk the plank: If someone walks the plank, they are going toward their own destruction or downfall

Walking encyclopedia: A very knowledgeable person is a walking encyclopedia.

Walking on air: If you are walking on air, you are so happy that you feel as if you could float.

Walking on broken glass: When a person is punished for something. e.g. 'She had me walking on broken glass.'

Walking time-bomb: A person whose behaviour is erratic and totally unpredictable is a walking time-bomb.

Wallflower: A woman politician given an unimportant government position so that the government can pretend it takes women seriously is a wallflower.

War chest: A war chest is a fund that can be used to finance a campaign like and election or for use in emergencies or unexpected times of difficulty.

Well-oiled machine: Something that functions very well is a well-oiled machine.

Were you born in a barn?: If someone asks you this, it means that you forgot to close the door when you came in.

When pigs fly: Meaning you will not get something when you want it or someone doesn't want something for you. say you are selling an item and some one doesn't want it. they might say 'I'll buy it when pigs fly'. it just means you will never get someone to say yes to you when you ask for something.

Whistle for it: If someone says that you can whistle for something, they are determined to ensure that you don't get it.

World is your oyster: When the world is your oyster, you are getting everything you want from life.

Wrong foot: If you start something on the wrong foot, you start badly.

X

X factor: The dangers for people in the military that civilians do not face, for which they receive payment, are known as the X factor.

X marks the spot: This is used to say where something is located or hidden.

X-rated: If something is x-rated, it is not suitable for children.

Y

Yah boo sucks: Yah boo & yah boo sucks can be used to show that you have no sympathy with someone.

Yank my chain: If some one says this to another person (i.e. stop yanking my chain) it means for the other person to leave the person who said it alone and to stop bothering them.

Young blood: Young people with new ideas and fresh approaches are young blood.

Young Turk: A Young Turk is a young person who is rebellious and difficult to control in a company, team or organisation.

Your belly button is bigger than your stomach: If your belly button is bigger than your stomach, you take on more responsibilities than you can handle.

Your call: If something is your call, it is up to you to make a decision on the matter.

Your name is mud: If someone's name is mud, then they have a bad reputation.

Your sins will find you out: This idiom means that things you do wrong will become known.

Z

Zero hour: The time when something important is to begin is zero hour.

Zero tolerance: If the police have a zero tolerance policy, they will not overlook any crime, no matter how small or trivial.

Zigged before you zagged: If you did things in the wrong order, you zigged before you zagged.

Zip it: This is used to tell someone to be quiet.

Zip your lip: If someone tells you to zip your lip, they want to to shut up or keep quiet about something.

Bibliography

Cambridge International Dictionary of Idioms and Phrases, (1998) Cambridge: Cambridge University Press.

Courtney, Rosemary (1983) *Longman Dictionary of Phrasal Verbs,* London: Longman.

Cowie, Anthony P.; and Mackin, Ronald (1975) *Oxford Dictionary of Current Idiomatic English Volume 1,* Oxford: Oxford University Press.

Cowie, Anthony P.; Mackin, Ronald; and McCaig, Isabel R.(1983) *Oxford Dictionary of Current Idiomatic English Volume 2,* Oxford: Oxford University Press.

Flavell, Linda; and Flavell, Roger (1993) *Dictionary of Idioms and their Origins,* London: Kyle Cathie.

Francis, Gill; Hunston, Susan; and Manning, Elizabeth (eds.) (1996) *Collins Cobuild Grammar Patterns 1: Verbs,* London: HarperCollins.

Gaffney, Sean; and Cashman, Seamus (1974) *Proverbs and Sayings of Ireland,* Dublin: Wolfhound Press.

Hendrickson, Robert (1987) *The Henry Holt Encyclopedia of Word and Phrase Origins,* New York: Henry Holt and Company.

Hill, Jimmie; and Lewis, Michael (eds.) (1997) *LTP Dictionary of Selected Collocations,* (edition of Kozlowska and Dzierzanowska 1982 and 1991) Hove: Language Teaching Publications.

Kjellmer, Göran (1994) *A Dictionary of English Collocations,* 3 volumes. Oxford: Clarendon Press.

Kozlowska, Christian D.; and Dzierzanowska, Halina (1988) *Selected English Collocations,* (2nd edition, 1993; 3rd edition, 1998) Warszawa: Wydawnictwo Naukowe PWN.

Lattey, Elsa; and Hieke, Adolf E. (1990) *Using Idioms in Situational Contexts: a Workbook,* Tübingen: Francke.

Long, Thomas Hill; and Summers, Della (eds.) (1979) *Longman Dictionary of English Idioms,* London: Longman.

Lubensky, Sophia (1995) *Random House Russian-English Dictionary of Idioms,* New York: Random House.

Makkai, Adam; Boatner, Maxine Tull; and Gates, John Edward (1995) *A Dictionary of American idioms,* (3rd edition) Hauppauge, NY: Barron's.

Manser, Martin H. (1985) *A Dictionary of Everyday Idioms,* (2nd edition, 1997, Prentice Hall) London: Macmillan.

__________ (1990) *Dictionary of Word and Phrase Origins,* London: Sphere Books.

Mieder, Wolfgang; Kingsbury, Stewart A.; and Harder, Kelsie B. (eds.) (1992) *A Dictionary of American Proverbs,* New York: Oxford University Press.

Moon, Rosamund (ed.) (1995) *Collins Cobuild Dictionary of Idioms,* London: HarperCollins.

Palmatier, Robert A.; and Ray, Harold L. (1993) *Dictionary of Sports Idioms,* Lincolnwood, Illinois: National Textbook Company.

Runcie, Moira (ed.) (2002) *Oxford Collocations Dictionary for Students of English,* Oxford: Oxford University Press.

Simpson, John A. (1992) *The Concise Oxford Dictionary of Proverbs,* (2nd edition) Oxford: Oxford University Press.

Sinclair, John M.; and Moon, Rosamund (eds.) (1989) *Collins Cobuild Dictionary of Phrasal Verbs,* London: HarperCollins.

Speake, Jennifer (2000) *The Oxford Dictionary of Idioms,* Oxford: Oxford University Press.

Spears, Richard A. (1994) *NTC's American Idioms Dictionary,* (2nd edition) Lincolnwood, Illinois: National Textbook Company.

Stern, Karen (ed.) (1998) *Longman Idioms Dictionary,* London: Longman.

Taylor, Ronald; and Gottschalk, Walter o.J. (1960) *A German-English Dictionary of Idioms. Idiomatic and Figurative Expressions with English Translations,* (4th edition) München: Max Hueber.

Urdang, Laurence; and Abate, Frank R. (eds.) (1983) *Idioms and Phrases Index,* (3 volumes) Gale Research Company.

Walter, Elizabeth; and Pye, Glennis (eds.) (1997) *Cambridge International Dictionary of Phrasal Verbs,* Cambridge: Cambridge University Press.

Walter, Elizabeth; and Pye, Glennis (eds.) (1998) *Cambridge International Dictionary of Phrasal Verbs: Anglais-Français,* Cambridge: Cambridge University Press.

Walter, Elizabeth; and Pye, Glennis (eds.)(1998) *Cambridge International Dictionary of Idioms,* Cambridge: Cambridge University Press.